POPE JOHN PAUL II
His Travels and Mission

Norman St John-Stevas is received by Pope John Paul II (From the author's collection)

Norman St John-Stevas

POPE
JOHN PAUL II

His Travels and Mission

faber and faber

First published in 1982
by Faber and Faber Limited
3 Queen Square London WC1N 3AU
Typeset by King's English Typesetters Limited, Cambridge
Printed in Spain by Heraclio Fournier S.A. Vitoria

British Library Cataloguing in Publication Data

St John-Stevas, Norman
Pope John Paul II: his travels and mission
1. *John Paul II, Pope*   2. *Popes – biography*
I. Title
282'.092'4   BX1378.5
ISBN 0-571-11908-5

Contents

Acknowledgements

———————— ✠ ————————

This is in no sense an official study of the travels and missions of John Paul II, and all opinions and assessments expressed are entirely my own, but I wish to place on record my gratitude to a number of people for their kindness to me. I am above all indebted to His Holiness himself for his generosity in receiving me in private audiences and for the privilege of attending the mass celebrated by him in his private chapel, which constituted for me a unique spiritual experience. I am also greatly indebted to Father John Magee, one of the Pope's principal private secretaries, for his acts of kindness. I would also like to thank Cardinal Casaroli, the Vatican Secretary of State, and Archbishop Van Lierde, Vicar General of the Vatican City, for their friendship extended to me over the years. My thanks too, to Bishop Agnellus Andrew, Padre Roberto Tucci, SJ, and Mr Peter Nichols for their advice about Vatican procedures.

Grateful acknowledgement is made to the following for permission to reproduce photographs: Associated Press, pages 19 (Cardinal Hume) and 86; British Tourist Authority, pages 15 and 18; Camera Press, pages 19 (Dr Runcie) and 59; Gianfranco Gorgoni/Contact/Colorific, page 42; Karsh of Ottawa, page 154; Keystone, page 111; Claus C. Meyer/Colorific, page 63 (top); National Portrait Gallery, pages 10, 11, and 14 (Cardinal Newman); Popperfoto, pages 14 (Pope John XXIII) and 23; Alon Reininger/Contact/Colorific, pages 38 and 94; Richard Romero/Colorific, page 63 (bottom). All other photographs, with the exception of the frontispiece and the photograph on page 26, are reproduced by kind permission of Carillon Publishing.

Acknowledgement is also made to Libreria Editrice Vaticana, Vatican City, and to the translator, Jerzy Peterkiewicz, for their kind permission to print extracts from Karol Wojtyla's *Easter Vigil and Other Poems*, published by Hutchinson and Co. (Publishers) Ltd.

1

The Pope in Britain

—————— ✠ ——————

On Friday, 28 May 1982, the papal jet will touch down in London, and history will be made. For the first time a reigning pope will be setting foot in Britain. The significance of the visit can hardly be overestimated. It can lay claim to be the most important ecclesiastical event that the nation has witnessed since the break with Rome by Henry VIII in 1534. That breach, temporarily healed by Queen Mary but confirmed by Queen Elizabeth I on her accession in 1559, was the decisive development in the Reformation struggle.

At the time it did not seem like that. England was a small, struggling country on the edge of Europe, insular and troublesome, but from Rome's point of view of only minor importance. Spain, by contrast, loomed large. Spain was the greatest Roman Catholic power of the period, bestriding the world with a great empire in the Americas and Africa, a country of incomparably greater significance than puny Britain. That is undoubtedly how it appeared to the sixteenth-century papacy, but Rome, not for the first time, was wrong.

Spain had already passed its zenith: the future belonged to England, a country just beginning an ascent in power and influence, both political and cultural, which was destined to continue unbroken for more than three centuries. This grand historical progress of increasing wealth and power was to be brought to an end only in the twentieth century under the impact of two world wars. Furthermore, it was from England that the North American continent was to be principally colonized. Thus, the culture of the nation destined to emerge as the greatest and most influential in the twentieth century, the United States, was to be overwhelmingly Protestant albeit with a strong and growing Catholic component.

Henry VIII (1491–1547)   Catherine of Aragon (1485–1536)

ROMAN CATHOLICISM IN BRITAIN

The far-off events of the sixteenth century meant that the identity of English culture and indeed of the English nation was to be indissolubly associated, if not with Protestantism as such, certainly with 'No Popery' and with anti-Roman attitudes. The national identity was to be established by conflict with the political and to a certain extent with the theological claims of Rome. Just as Irish nationalism identified itself with Catholicism so English nationalism drew strength from its Protestant foundations. The Catholic religion was proscribed, recusants were fined, and until Catholic emancipation in 1829, Roman Catholics were debarred from any kind of office or service in public life.

Of course, Catholicism remained a part of English culture: the Church of England was never the Presbyterian Kirk, and it was its proud boast to be both Catholic and reformed. Elizabeth I and the Stuarts after her were determined that Anglicanism should be a *via media*, but it was a *via media* with a decisive turn against Rome. Thus it was that many of the symbols that we think of as being peculiarly English, such as the cathedrals, the great parish churches, Parliament and indeed the Crown, although retaining their Catholic ethos were severed from their Roman roots. It was only in the nineteenth century that the Oxford Movement, pursuing the logic of its own Catholic principles, ended up by reverting to Rome. In so doing, it entered a national cul-de-sac and even today the lasting influence of the Oxford Movement is to be seen more in the Church of England than in the Church of Rome.

When the Roman Catholic hierarchy was restored in England in 1850, the resultant anti-Roman outbreaks that led Parliament to pass the foolish and unenforceable Ecclesiastical Titles Act, forbidding Catholic prelates to use their titles under the threat of heavy penalties, showed that 'No Popery' was still an intrinsic part of English culture.

Yet there were signs of a change. Walter Bagehot, the nineteenth century's most perceptive critic, noted the strength of the anti-papal feeling in Britain in the 1850s but treated it with a note of detachment and mockery which heralded

Sir Thomas More (1478–1535)

Bishop John Fisher (1469–1535)

11

changes to come. 'Tell an Englishman that a building is without use', he wrote in 1852 in his essay on Oxford, 'and he will stare; that it is illiberal, and he will survey it; that it teaches Aristotle, and he will seem perplexed that it don't teach science, and he won't mind; but only hint that it is the Pope, and he will arise and burn it to the ground.' Even better is his treatment of Gibbon's conversion to Catholicism in the previous century. 'It seems now so natural that an Oxford man should take this step', he wrote, 'that one can hardly understand the astonishment it created. Lord Sheffield tells us that the Privy Council interfered; and with good administrative judgement examined a London bookseller—some Mr Lewis who had no concern in it. In the Manor house of Buriton it would have created less sensation if *dear Edward* had announced his intention of becoming a monkey. The English have ever believed that the Papist is a kind of *creature*; and every sound mind would prefer a beloved child to produce a tail, a hide of hair, and a taste for nuts, in comparison with transubstantiation, wax candles and belief in the glories of Mary.'

The English have long suffered from a temperamental incapacity for absolutes but the one metaphysical principle which the people have been able to imbibe is to be against the pope. Cardinal Newman maintained that with regard to Catholicism English people bore a stain upon their imagination, an intrinsic part of that stain being the concept of the papacy. History, whatever Henry Ford may have thought, is far from bunk, and there is no doubt that for some people the papal visit will present an insurmountable psychological obstacle. It is, however, a measure of the changes that have taken place in the British view of the papacy in recent years that they will find themselves in a tiny minority.

Royal visits to the Vatican have helped to bring about a change of attitude, the latest being a state visit paid by the Queen and Prince Philip to Pope John Paul on 17 October 1980. The Pope, wearing the stole which he dons for the visits of the heads of other Churches, paid tribute to the Queen and singled out 'the great simplicity and dignity with which Your Majesty bears the weight of your responsibilities'. In return Her Majesty expressed her pleasure at the Pope's forthcoming visit to Britain and gave the first royal commendation of the ecumenical movement.

Only twenty years ago a papal visit to Britain would have been unthinkable. One reason, of course, was that popes had given up the habit of travelling outside Rome. But even if they had reacquired the habit of foreign travel at that time, England would have been virtually the last country that any pope would have thought of visiting. How has it come about that English attitudes have changed so fundamentally? First of all, the rise of Soviet Communism has undoubtedly led many in England to see the papacy in a different light, more as a defence of civilization and traditional values than as a threat to them. Secondly the ecumenical movement on a world-wide basis has led to a softening of historical asperities: faced with a rising tide of secularism and materialism Christians have been impelled to move closer together. Ecumenism, starting in the Protestant world, spread to the heart of Catholicism at Rome through the Second Vatican Council. There is no doubt that the majority of Protestants and Catholics see historical disputes over theological dogmas in a new perspective and have appreciated that the things which unite the Christian Churches are more important than those that divide them.

ECUMENISM TODAY

As far as the ecumenical movement of Britain is concerned, Pope John Paul II's visit will mark a new milestone in the record of reconciliation between the Churches, and in particular the *rapprochement* between Canterbury and Rome. Primarily the papal visit is made to the Roman Catholic community in Britain, but it is to its ecumenical impact that we must look if we are to assess its lasting significance. (Technically the Pope is meant to reply to propositions put forward by the Liverpool Pastoral Congress of May 1980 but their radical suggestions are unlikely to evoke a favourable response.) The Pope's visit is a direct descendant of that made by Dr Geoffrey Fisher, then Archbishop of Canterbury, to the Vatican to see Pope John XXIII two decades ago in 1960, the first such visit since Archbishop Arundel went to Rome in 1397.

It would be difficult to think of a less likely prelate to have made that historic breakthrough than the schoolmasterly, slightly pedantic, distinctly Protestant Dr Fisher, yet it was he who had the vision to respond wholeheartedly and uncalculatingly to the opportunities opened up by Pope John. Pope John will surely be seen as the greatest pope of the twentieth century: the caretaker pope elected in the autumn of 1958 who proceeded to turn the Church upside down by calling the Second Vatican Council; the pope who, by the transcendance of his charity, his understanding and care for all human beings, his profound yet enigmatic words, is the pontiff of modern times who most resembles Christianity's founder.

I was in Rome for the meeting with Archbishop Fisher and was able to observe at first hand the consternation of the Vatican and its officials at the arrival of their historic visitor. The popular press grasped early the significance of the event and it was headlined in the *Daily Mirror* as 'The Holy Summit'. Dr Fisher was received in the Vatican with all the enthusiasm accorded to a germ in a maternity ward. The Vatican paper *L'Osservatore Romano* was uncertain even what to call him. Photographs of the event, which are normally freely allowed, were forbidden; the Vatican Press Office was almost totally obstructive but the qualities of the two participants overcame all obstacles. Dr Fisher remained

Cardinal John Newman (1801–90)   Pope John XXIII

serene, practical and very English; Pope John's warmth and love swept away any hitches in protocol. Dr Fisher's first words as he swept into the papal study on that bright and hopeful December day were: 'Your Holiness, we are making history.' The actual conversation between the Pope and the Archbishop was shrouded in secrecy but at a press conference later in the day at the British Embassy Dr Fisher lifted the hem of the iron curtain and stressed the cordiality of the encounter.

I was present at the press conference and raised the question of how the two ecclesiastics greeted each other. The Archbishop answered that they greeted each other as any two clerics would in such circumstances, 'in the ordinary friendly way', and we deduced that there had been no kissing of rings but that they had shaken hands. Dr Fisher then provided a little verbal embroidery. 'There was no preliminary build up,' he said, 'no theatrical staging; it was nothing like visiting Hitler or Mussolini'! At these words I saw the Holy Summit going up in smoke, but the Archbishop's resourceful press officer, Colonel

Canterbury Cathedral

Westminster Cathedral

Hornby, jumped to his feet and uttered the words 'Off the record, I presume, Your Grace', and off the record they have remained until today.

The evening before the papal audience there had been evensong at All Saints, the preposterous little Victorian Gothic Anglican church in the Via Babuino, and after the service I was able to greet the Archbishop, offering words of welcome and discharging a mandate which I certainly had not received. 'On behalf of English Roman Catholics I welcome you to Rome, Your Grace, and I hope and pray that this may be the first move towards the reunion of the Anglican and Roman Catholic Churches.' These were prophetic words but Dr Fisher, who had a practical turn of mind, when he had got over his astonishment, replied simply: 'Thank you very much, but your hierarchy will have to catch up with you.'

There had been quite a lot of 'catching up' by the time Dr Ramsey visited Rome in 1966 and was accorded all the honours of a prince of the Church. There was even a joint ecumenical service at St Paul's-outside-the-Walls in which both Paul VI and Dr Ramsey took part. The Church of England was raised from the somewhat grudging technical status of an 'ecclesial community' to—in the words of the Pope—'a sister Church'.

The fruits of Pope Paul's generosity will be reaped when the present pope visits Canterbury in June for a service which will be conducted by the Archbishop of Canterbury, and it is hoped that the Pope will give the address. This could be the occasion for the Pope to announce the further revision of the laws on mixed marriages and the re-opening of the question of the validity of Anglican orders.

Canterbury is likely to provide the high point of the papal visit. The Pope will not only be following in the footsteps of Chaucer in visiting the tomb of St Thomas of Canterbury, but be going to the heart of the Anglican community. (And how suitable it would be if His Holiness took the opportunity to restore the Feast of St Thomas to the calendar of the Universal Church from which it was recently removed. The devotion to St Thomas in medieval times was of European dimensions—his likeness is included for example in the mosaics of Monreale in Sicily.) Dr Runcie is not only Archbishop of Canterbury but head of the Anglican Communion throughout the world. Anglicanism followed the British flag but the flag has gone and the Anglican Church remains with every claim to be considered a religious body of major international importance.

While at Canterbury the Pope will hold conversations not only with Anglicans but with representatives of the Free Churches and other Churches in Britain. Both Dr Runcie and Cardinal Hume have looked forward to union between their two Churches in their own lifetimes, and the Pope's visit is likely to give a new impetus to the ecumenical tide. As a *Times* leading article put it on 1 September 1980, after the papal visit had been announced: 'Most Christians in Britain regard their divisions as scandalous and disgraceful, and are anxious to see a rapid and continuous development of the ecumenical movement. To this, the Pope's visit must make a major contribution.'

POPE JOHN PAUL II ACCEPTS THE INVITATION

A papal visit to Britain has long been mooted, indeed there was considerable speculation in the popular press about the possibility of a visit by Paul VI shortly after his accession to the papacy, but nothing came of it. With the accession of John Paul II and his inauguration of a series of papal journeys, speculation about his coming to Britain increased, and I raised the matter with the Pope when I was received in private audience by him on 24 May 1980. I was able to tell the Holy Father how welcome he would be in Britain, how the bonds between Poland and Britain were particularly strong, and that therefore a Polish pope would in many ways be the ideal person to open a new era of good relations between Britain and the Vatican. My suggestion was favourably received and the Holy Father made it plain that were an invitation for him to visit Britain to be issued, it would be given favourable consideration. He left me in no doubt that he was not interested in a state visit to Britain as such but in a visit of primarily pastoral concern.

The official invitation was issued by Cardinal Hume and Archbishop Worlock in September of the same year when during an audience with the Pope they presented him with a copy of *The Easter People*, the response of the English bishops to the National Pastoral Congress which had been held in Liverpool in the spring. The Pastoral Congress was the first representative meeting of the English Catholic laity to have taken place, and it came up with a number of controversial recommendations to which the bishops have given a cautious response. No view on these has come from the Pope but this visit to Britain could be the obvious occasion for some papal pronouncement to be made.

The invitation from the English bishops was immediately followed by a further invitation from Cardinal Gray on behalf of the Scottish bishops for a papal visit to Scotland. The Archbishop of Canterbury who had already been consulted about the visit followed this up with an invitation to visit Canterbury. Dr Runcie had in fact met the Pope in Ghana in May 1980 when, by chance, both were visiting Africa. He had indicated to the Pope that he would be most welcome to come to Canterbury should he in fact pay a visit to Britain.

The Pope swiftly accepted the invitation of the Catholic bishops and his decision was announced at a press conference held in London on 31 August 1980. Cardinal Hume declared: 'I am delighted that Pope John Paul II has agreed to make a pastoral visit to the Roman Catholic community of England and Wales and that he has accepted a similar invitation to visit the Roman Catholics of

Martyrdom of Thomas of Canterbury

Dr Runcie,
Archbishop of
Canterbury

Cardinal
Basil Hume

Scotland. The Pope's chief concern will be to remind our Roman Catholic community of our duty and responsibility to live more faithfully and more fully the gospel message of Jesus Christ. Pope John Paul is particularly anxious that the ecumenical aspect of his visit be handled sensitively and to good effect. He will come to our country as a friend, and, as in all his pastoral visits, bring a message of encouragement, hope and peace. I sincerely hope that all our countrymen will be able to share the joy of the Roman Catholic community.'

The decision for the papal visit to be a pastoral rather than a state occasion was undoubtedly wise. At a stroke it cut through any constitutional difficulties that might have arisen owing to the Queen's position as head of the Established Church. The Queen herself, it is understood, not only had no objection to the visit but positively welcomed it. She is known to have been deeply impressed by the papal visit to Poland in 1979 and by the sight of the cross, the supreme symbol of the Christian faith, erected in the centre of the Communist capital of Warsaw. During the visit the Pope will call on the Queen and other members of the royal family. At one time I had hoped that the Pope would be invited to address both Houses of Parliament, but although this would have been acceptable to the Speaker and others responsible for the Palace of Westminster, it unfortunately did not find favour with the present government.

The announcement of the papal visit was generally welcomed in both secular and church circles, even the evangelical *Church Society* giving it a qualified welcome. Opposition came, as was to be expected, from certain militant Protestants, including the Reverend Ian Paisley and some churchmen in Scotland, but the Presbyterian Church, the Established Church of Scotland, welcomed the visit and authorized its head, the Moderator, to meet the Pope when he arrived. Mr Enoch Powell produced a recondite argument that it would be unconstitutional for the Pope to set foot in Britain but this was regarded more as a curiosity than as a major contribution to the debate.

Pope John Paul II is certainly the pope who has evoked the greatest interest and admiration in Britain. His courage, vigour and leadership have been widely welcomed and the affection and respect for him were greatly increased by the assassination attempt of 1981. The Pope is now recognized as a representative of a spiritual not a temporal power, and a man who sums up in his charismatic person, aspirations for peace and goodwill which are the common property of mankind.

PAPAL VISIT LTD

During his five-day visit the Pope will visit not only England but Wales and Scotland, and a number of religious ceremonies will take place including an open-air mass in Wembley Stadium. Naturally the uncertainty of the Pope's health has meant that the arrangements for the visit have had to remain flexible, and greater emphasis is likely to be placed on the transmission of his pastoral message by the broadcasting media than in any other of his foreign visits.

The cost of the visit will be high and is estimated to be in the region of several million pounds. Monsignor Ralph Brown of Westminster Cathedral has been charged with the duty of organizing the visit and has engaged the services of the American entrepreneur Mr Mark McCormack, who, in return for a licence to sell and distribute authorized souvenirs, will be entitled to a percentage commission of 20 per cent. Papal Visit Ltd will not be to everyone's taste but it is difficult to see how money on this scale could be raised without some kind of arrangement of this kind. Authorized souvenirs will bear a logo made up of a cross, and traces of the Union flag, centred around the papal crossed keys. The colours of the logo will be blue, the colour of Our Lady, and gold, the papal colour. Apart from the expense of security arrangements, no cost will fall upon the general public. This seems both sensible and desirable and has precluded the chance of the visit being marred by a new version of the old cry of 'Rome on the rates'.

2

The Popes Take Off

Pope John Paul's visit to Britain must be seen in the context of his programme of world-wide travel, of which the British visit is the latest instalment. During his three-year reign he has made no less than ten major journeys—to Latin America, Poland, Ireland, the United States, Turkey, Africa, France, Brazil, Germany and Asia. Had it not been for the assassination attempt in Rome in May 1981 there would also have been visits to Lourdes and Switzerland, but these have had to be postponed.

Besides his international visits, Pope John Paul has travelled widely in Italy. Most of these visits have been in the nature of pilgrimages: to Turin for example to see the Holy Shroud; to Siena to pay honour to St Catherine; to Monte Cassino to visit the Tomb of St Benedict; to Loreto to visit the Holy House; to Pompeii and to Naples; and finally to Bergamo in April 1981, for the celebrations marking the centenary of the birth of John XXIII. The Pope has also made numerous sorties from the Vatican into Rome, visiting amongst other places, the Polish College, the English College, and the Gregorian University. He has also paid a series of visits to Roman parishes, carrying out inspections in his capacity as Bishop of Rome.

THE TRAVELS OF POPE PAUL VI

John Paul's travels are a continuation, a confirmation and an intensification of those of his predecessor, Paul VI. Pope Paul must be regarded as the founder of the tradition of world-wide travel as part of the papal ministry. He too carried out ten major visits during his pontificate, including those to the Holy Land, India, Australia, and the United States, before advancing age and ill-health prevented his travelling again. Although his visits did not make the popular

'Popemobile', France 1980

Pope Paul VI

impact of the present pope, they were profoundly important in developing the role of the modern papacy.

I was in the Holy Land in January 1964 for the first foreign visit of a pope in modern times. Fighting his way up the packed Via Dolorosa in Jerusalem, with only one unscheduled halt at the convent of the nuns of Our Lady of Sion, Pope Paul became the first pope ever to have visited the Holy Sepulchre. The scene was extraordinary. As I wrote at the time: 'Beneath the crumbling, peeling dome of the Church of the Holy Sepulchre, wild confusion reigned. Cameramen and Italian television technicians, who had monopoly coverage, swarmed every-where. Some clung to the scaffolding, others poked their cameras through the candlesticks on the tinselly altar set up by the Franciscans. Some were even perched on the shrine of the Holy Sepulchre itself. Patriarchs, bishops, monsignori and high Vatican and Jerusalem officials were crammed together in an undignified gaggle at the side of the altar, fighting for every foothold. Friars, police and legionaries shouted, pushed and struggled. Above their heads the string of electric lightbulbs suspended to supplement the cluster of smoky oil lamps fused and burst into flames. The tightly packed crowd mercifully failed to panic, and the leaping flames were beaten out with a bedouin head-dress hoisted into position on a silver-topped patriarchal stave. Throughout it all, Pope Paul maintained an unshakeable dignity. Rapt and exalted, he celebrated mass before the Tomb.' (*Economist*, 11 January 1964)

One major effect of the visit was visibly to re-establish the papacy as a world spiritual authority, moving it out of the baroque background of Rome into the Christological setting of the Holy Land itself. Furthermore, by his bold initiative, the Pope had ranged himself symbolically on the side of the forces making for change and renewal within the Catholic Church. The conservatives in the Curia took the point and started a grumbling, which continues today, suggesting that the dignity and prestige of the papacy were being impaired.

Equally important at the time were the ecumenical aspects of the visit. Jerusalem was the scene of the first meeting between a pope and a patriarch of Constantinople, Athenagoras, since the East–West schism of 900 years before. The Patriarch Athenagoras addressed the Pope as 'the first Bishop of the Church', a revolutionary public recognition of the Roman primacy. The Pope in his address at Bethlehem responded in kind, declaring: 'We shall put our trust in prayer which, even though it is not yet a united prayer, rises up, nevertheless, simultaneously from ourselves and from Christians separated from us, like two parallel columns which meet on high to form an arch.' Almost equally significant was the exchange of visits between the Pope and Patriarch Benedictos, the Orthodox Patriarch of Jerusalem, constituting another step in the reconciliation of Rome and the Orthodox Church as well as a softening of the rivalries between them over the control of the Holy Places in Jerusalem itself.

Pope Paul followed up this visit with others. The most notable was his journey to the United Nations headquarters in New York in October 1965. The sight of the slim, white-and-scarlet-robed figure walking the length of the great blue and gold assembly hall of the United Nations was unforgettable. The Pope put the full weight of his office behind the United Nations, saying: 'It is the world's greatest hope. It is, we presume to say, the reflection of the loving and transcendent design of God for the progress of the human family on earth.' He then addressed himself to the problems of world poverty, stressing that the gulf between the rich and poor nations had to be bridged, but he struck a discordant note in his unexpected condemnation of contraception. Dealing with the subject of disarmament, he called on the nations to give up 'offensive' weapons while admitting the necessity to retain 'defensive' ones until an international order was created that guaranteed security without recourse to arms. The most moving moment in the address came with the Pope's impassioned appeal for peace. Quoting President Kennedy's words, 'Mankind must put an end to war, or war will put an end to mankind', the Pope added in ringing tones: 'No more war, war never again! Never one against the other, or even one above the other, but always, on every occasion, with each other.'

Pope Paul was the pontiff destined actually to launch the modern phase of papal travel, but the idea—like so many other innovating ideas—originally came from John XXIII. It was Pope John who planned the visit to Jerusalem but he died before his purpose could be accomplished. Yet already he had broken a 100-year-old tradition when on 4 October 1962 he left the Vatican in the papal train, never before used this century, to make a pilgrimage to Assisi and Loreto, just a week before the Second Vatican Council was due to open.

PAPAL TRAVEL THROUGH THE CENTURIES

Papal travel, in fact, has had a chequered history and has frequently reflected the changing fortunes of the papacy itself. St Peter—the first Bishop of Rome—was a notable itinerant, moving from Jerusalem to Antioch, and finally to Rome itself where he met a martyr's death. In the sixth and seventh centuries a number of popes visited Constantinople, some willingly like John I, others not so freely, like Martin I, who was abducted and eventually died in exile in the Crimea. In the Middle Ages popes left Rome at intervals on a variety of missions. Leo III (795–816) went to Padaborn to obtain support from Charlemagne; Stephen V (816–17) crossed the Alps to meet the Emperor Louis the Pius at Rheims; both Benedict VIII (1012–24) and Leo IX (1049–54) paid visits to Germany. In the fourteenth century Clement V (1305–14) removed himself to France despairing of the turbulence of Rome, and eventually moved the papacy

A contemporary print showing Pope Pius VII (1800–23) levitating while in jail – a novel mode of papal travel! (From the author's collection)

to Avignon. The Great Schism followed and it was not until the reign of Gregory XI (1370–8) that the papacy was moved back to Rome.

The Avignon experience undoubtedly discouraged the popes from going abroad, and there were no more such visits until Pius VI (1775–84) visited Vienna for talks with the Emperor Joseph II. The balcony in Vienna from which he gave the blessing *Urbi et Orbi* can still be seen. Later he paid an enforced visit to France when he was captured by Napoleon and taken off as a prisoner. His successor Pius VII (1800–23) went to Paris voluntarily for the coronation of Napoleon in 1804, but—in a memorable gesture—Napoleon snatched the crown out of his hand and crowned himself. Later he returned to France involuntarily as a prisoner in 1809 having excommunicated Napoleon for his annexation of the papal states.

Pius IX, elected in 1846, might well have proved a redoubtable papal traveller had not the events of history turned against him. Shortly after his election he planned to introduce railways into the papal states, he inaugurated governmental reforms, and was hailed by Jowett of Balliol as 'a capital fellow'. Metternich, dismayed, declared that he had allowed for everything except a liberal pope. Pio Nono's liberalism came to an end in November 1848 when Rossi, the papal Prime Minister, was murdered on the steps of the Cancelleria in Rome. The Pope fled to Gaeta, carrying the Blessed Sacrament with him in the ciborium used by Pius VI when carried off captive to France by Napoleon. Pius IX's companions on being informed by the Pope of his illustrious burden tried to fall to their knees, almost upsetting the carriage.

In 1850 the Pope was back in Rome, taking up residence in the Vatican and abandoning the traditional palace of the popes in the Quirinale. Ten years later he paid a visit to Civita Vecchia on his own new railway line, travelling in state in a train (still to be seen in the Museum of Rome) which contained a drawing room, a dressing room and a private chapel. Apart from this journey Pio Nono confined himself to walking in Rome—the long struggle between himself and Cavour and Garibaldi over the future of Rome and the papal states made further travelling impossible.

On 19 September 1870 Pio Nono made his last journey through the eternal city to St John Lateran, his cathedral church, where he mounted the *Scala Santa* on his knees, and turned to give a final blessing to his troops. This was the last public act of a pope in papal Rome. On 20 September the bombardment of the city began. The Pope ordered the offering of only token resistance and on the same day the white flag flew from the cupola of St Peter's. Pio Nono withdrew into his palace and became 'the prisoner in the Vatican'. The popes were to remain voluntary prisoners there until the signing of the Lateran Treaty of 1929 between Italy and the Holy See put an end to the Roman Question. After that the popes did venture out into Rome but it was not until Pope John's reign that a pope once again left the confines of the eternal city.

THE PURPOSE OF JOHN PAUL'S TRAVELS

The apostles were commanded by the Lord himself to go and teach all nations (Matthew 28:19). St Paul in his turn was indefatigable in his journeys around the Mediterranean and the Roman Empire. The purpose of apostolic travels was to spread the gospel and it is this which remains the prime impulse behind papal travel today. As the Pope himself said at the end of his visit to Brazil, his presence as pope was to manifest Christ to people everywhere. This Christological foundation to the Pope's travelling cannot be overemphasized, any more than the concept can be exaggerated as the foundation of his whole thought.

(See, for example, his first encyclical, *Redemptor Hominis*.) For the Pope, the Incarnation is *the* great event, changing the course of world history and giving meaning and understanding to the life of man. He sees his travels as a manifestation of Christ and a living declaration of Christian witness, and it is this spiritual foundation which has given them their impact. What the people are responding to is not only a spectacle but the presence of the spiritual in their midst.

The Pope has the gift of remaining faithful to his own Christian vision and at the same time evoking a spiritual response in people of very different traditions and formations. In his addresses he continually insists, and did so most notably in his address to UNESCO in Paris, that there is an intrinsic link between Christianity, culture and man's spiritual nature. In Paris he concluded his UNESCO address by calling for a new effort to bring about a recognition of the priority of the ethical over the technical, and of the spiritual over the material nature of human endeavours. This spiritual message is mediated through the Pope's own natural gifts, his warmth, his humanity, his openness, his handsome and vigorous appearance, and his ability to project both personality and message, all of which can be summed up in a single word, his 'charisma'.

The second purpose of the papal voyages is to bring the pope to the people as a person. Despite all the developments of modern travel, only a tiny minority of the world's population can hope to see the pope in Rome. They do this, of course, and in increasing numbers. One of the features of this pontificate has been the extraordinary increase in the numbers travelling to Rome to see Pope John Paul. The weekly general audience, sufficient for all his predecessors, had first to be doubled, then trebled, then repeated on other days of the week, then shifted out of Paul VI's hideous new audience chamber into St Peter's basilica, and finally, when even this huge church was crowded out, moved into the Piazza San Pietro itself. Enthusiasm for the Pope in Rome scales ever new heights. Nuns in Rome are a notoriously fierce breed, but this must be the first time that a tribe of them has pulled every button off the papal cassock! Metternich was disconcerted by the emergence of a liberal pope, but what would he have made of an even stranger manifestation—a pop pope?

The response of the people, evidenced by their presence in huge numbers, their enthusiasm, and their exuberance, has marked all his ten major journeys, with only two exceptions, those to the basically non-Christian cultures of Turkey and Japan. In both, furthermore, the tight security arrangements contributed to a damping down of the ardour of the welcome. The people are responding both to the man and to the spiritual force he embodies. No doubt the Pope is a celebrity, a kind of religious pop star and this evokes its own response, but nobody who has witnessed any of the visits can doubt that there is more to it than that.

Above all, the Pope has an extraordinary appeal for youth. This was seen most clearly in Ireland where a whole generation responded. They sang their songs to him, 'He has the whole world in his arms', and he responded in uninhibited terms, 'Young people of Ireland, I love you.' It was the same story earlier in Poland, later in the United States, and subsequently in both France and Germany. This response of youth to the Pope tells us something important about his message: it is not addressed to the present, much less is it a harking back to the past, even when it is most severe; the Pope is always addressing the future and the generations which are to come.

As a result of these journeys and the Pope's self-projection he has become not only a world leader, but the outstanding world leader of our time. I was able to forecast this development in an article I wrote for the *Observer* on 6 May 1979, just before the last British general election. 'Pope John Paul comes to the chair of Peter when there is something like a vacuum in world leadership which he might well be able to fill. Chairman Mao is gone; Mr Brezhnev is probably dying and his colleagues are preoccupied with the problems of the succession; in the West President Carter has proved less than charismatic, and the European countries have failed to produce statesmen of the immediate post war calibre: the Pope has a unique opportunity to provide moral leadership not only for Catholics nor even for Christians but for all mankind.'

The Pope himself is fully aware of his world role. On his way back to Rome from France in 1980 he pointed out that the horizon both of the Church and of man 'expands continually and requires the pope to make himself present everywhere . . . It is to confirm the Christian faith and promote these values that the pope travels on the pathways of the world.'

Pope John Paul consciously uses his foreign visits to express his mind on the great issues of the day. Every visit has been accompanied by a flood of addresses and sermons, sometimes as many as fifty in number. All are written not by curial officials but by the Pope himself. He prepares for his visits in the greatest detail, and before embarking on a visit to a particular country studies carefully the social, religious and political conditions prevailing. He sees his visits as a manifestation of 'collegiality in the Church', a term meaning that the Catholic bishops share responsibility for governing the Church with the pope and are not merely papal agents. In his address to the Roman Curia on 28 June 1980 he declared that his journeys were 'an authentic pilgrimage to the sanctuary of God' and constituted an expression of 'collegiality in action'.

The bishops of the country he is to visit are closely consulted before his arrival. They are requested to forward to him full accounts of the problems facing their local Churches and, if possible, a meeting is arranged with representatives of the bishops before the papal visit takes place. In this way the Curia is often bypassed and a form of collegiality established which was certainly never originally

The Pope has an extraordinary appeal for the young people of every country that he visits

The travelling pope,
France 1980

Speaking at Fulda, Germany
1980

envisaged when the idea first came into vogue at the Second Vatican Council. There is, however, another side to the coin: the journeys can be a way of reasserting papal authority over the local Churches.

Certain themes are naturally common to all the papal visits but it is possible to discern a particular pattern in each of the different visits. Thus, in his first visit to address the South American bishops in Mexico in early 1979, the Pope was at pains to establish a balance between the duty of the Church and its leaders to work for the alleviation of the lot of the poor and the establishment of social justice, and the need for the Church to remain faithful to its purely spiritual message. In Poland, the Pope stressed the inviolable nature of the human person and his rights to liberty of conscience. In Ireland the theme which emerged as dominant was the condemnation of violence. In the United States he reasserted the traditional disciplines of the Church against the excesses of the consumer society. In Turkey he was at pains to advance good relations between the Catholic and Orthodox Churches. In Africa, while admiring the vitality of African Catholicism he warned that Africanization should not be carried too far. In Germany he stressed the common heritage of Protestants and Catholics. In Asia his dominant themes were the duty to work for social justice and the paramount need of preserving peace.

The Pope's lofty motives for pursuing a world-travel policy are undoubtedly reinforced by psychological and political factors. By basing himself on widespread popular support he has established a position of independence in relation to the Curia. He has an intense desire to see things for himself. Long before he became pope he had travelled to North America, the Far East and also widely in western Europe, despite the restrictions imposed on him as a Polish citizen. In many ways he needs psychologically to escape from the Vatican. He would have great sympathy with Pope John's anguished statement, *'sono nello sacco qui'*—they have got me in the bag here. The Pope has a strongly extrovert side to his personality. He enjoys exercise, mountaineering, hiking and physical activity. On arriving at the Vatican he wished to install a swimming pool in the papal apartments, but was restrained from doing so by curial arguments about the danger of leaks on to the priceless frescos in the rooms below! He had to content himself in this instance with a swimming pool installed in his summer residence at Castel Gandolfo. Undoubtedly he feels a great homesickness for his native soil and this can to some extent be assuaged by constant exits from the Vatican. Nor should it be forgotten that the Pope is very much an actor who responds to crowds. He trained as an actor in his youth and like so many great leaders seems to draw strength from actual contact with the people. The journeys provide an outlet for his restless energy.

Inevitably, the intensive programme of papal travel has aroused criticism, and from two distinct sources. On the one hand liberal Catholics have regretted the exaltation of the papacy which the phenomenally successful journeys have inevitably brought in their wake. It seems that at a stroke—or at least at a series of them—the Pauline conciliar papacy has been demolished and the old triumphalist papacy of Pius XII has returned. This same group criticizes the Pope for laying down the law too heavily on his visits and not listening enough to the point of view of those he has come to lead. There is not much evidence of any real dialogue or exchange of views during the packed itineraries and whirlwind visits which take place. Fears have also been expressed that local politicians take advantage of papal visits for their own ends. Particular anxiety was aroused by the Pope's visit to the Philippines and to Brazil. In his book *The Pope's Divisions* (Faber, 1981), Peter Nichols, the Rome correspondent of *The Times*, records that a number of Philippine Catholics had come to the conclusion that they would be better off without a papal visit. Indeed a group of nuns wrote to the organizers giving their reasons for doubting the value of such a descent. First, they feared that the papal presence could strengthen the authoritarian regime of the President and Mrs Marcos and they were also anxious that the Pope's conservatism might assist the reactionaries in the country. In the event these fears proved unjustified. The Pope made it clear to the presidential pair that the preservation of human rights was of paramount importance, and in Brazil he was equally forthright in his utterances.

Certain members of the Curia have expressed opposition to the journeys from a different point of view. Those who go on these journeys feel they are overshadowed by the papal presence and are transformed into nullities whom nobody wants to see or talk to. Those who stay at home feel that the administration of the Church suffers by the long absences. Business builds up, documents accumulate, and there is a danger of the system seizing up. Such criticism has some substance. Of all bureaucratic systems, the papal one is most dependent upon one man; and just as a secular ministerial system tends to malfunction in the absence of a minister, so a similar effect, much magnified, attends the absence of the pope.

Pope John Paul is aware of these criticisms and in June 1980, in an interview given to the Vatican paper *L'Osservatore Romano*, he noted: 'Many people say the Pope is travelling too much and at too frequent intervals. Speaking from the human point of view, they are right.' But the Pope went on to say that in undertaking what some people might consider excessive travel, he was in fact guided by Providence. Against such a papal ploy there can be no appeal. A less telling argument used by curialists is that the mystique of the papacy is in fact reduced by foreign availability; they suggest that people should come to the pope rather than the pope go to them.

Mass at Cologne,
Germany 1980

Another papal arrival

The Popes Take Off

THE POPE'S JOURNEYS IN THE FUTURE

What of papal travel in the future? Undoubtedly it has drawbacks as well as advantages. The scale of the papal visits is such as to impose heavy expenses on the host countries. There is some parallel to the visits which Queen Elizabeth I paid round the counties in sixteenth-century England. They delighted her county hosts but frequently beggared them as well. A further question can be raised: what will happen when the Pope runs out of places to go to? This is not an entirely unserious point, though with European countries such as Spain and Portugal as yet unvisited, with many countries in Africa in the same condition, and with no visits as yet paid either to India or to China there seems to be plenty of scope for papal travel for years to come.

A more serious obstacle to further papal journeys was created by the assassination attempt in May 1981. Until then, the punishing itineraries of the papal journeys had been tolerable to a pope who was in robust health. In future the strain is likely to be considerably greater. Furthermore, there is a psychological factor which has to be considered. Although the assassination attempt took place in St Peter's Square, it was at one of those mass audiences which the Pope has instituted in the open air in Rome in order to show himself to the maximum number of people. It is now understood that the Pope has gone through a period of self-questioning as to whether the attempt was a sign that God wishes this part of the papal ministry to be curtailed. There is also the more practical issue of whether the journeys will lay him open to further assassination attempts. As we have seen in the United States, there is an imitative factor in these attacks. Perhaps the most likely development is that the papal journeys will go on but that they will be less frequent, and that they may be of a less spectacular public character. The Pope could make much greater use of the media of television and broadcasting when visiting a country in order to communicate with the mass of the people. This would have been a natural development of papal travels in any event, and the assassination attempt may well have advanced it.

3

Pope John Paul's Ten Journeys

MEXICO

The Pope's first visit abroad came within a few months of his election when he set off for Mexico in late January 1979, arriving there on 27 January to address the General Assembly of Latin American Bishops meeting at Puebla the following day. A papal visit had been long expected but twice postponed—first because of the ill-health of Paul VI, and then through the untimely death of his successor John Paul I.

No more appropriate place could be found than Latin America to begin the cycle of papal travels. Latin America in a very real sense is the Catholic continent of the future. Half of the world's Catholic population resides in it and the Church there is facing some of the most intractable problems of our times. Catholics and their leaders have to bridge the gulf between rich and poor which has fissured the social fabric of every Latin American country. All these countries are facing massive population growth, with abortion still the principal means of population control. The situation has been graphically summed up by Peter Nichols when he writes in *The Pope's Divisions* that Latin America 'is a huge zone of oppression and traditional injustice, exploited economically, despised politically, feared for the dreadful object-lessons it provides of what happens to the human race when the social structure is unjust, breeding terrorism and huge inhuman cities and, as well as all this, it is almost entirely Catholic.' (p.321)

Throughout Latin America the Catholic Church finds itself faced with a dilemma, whether to use its power and influence to oppose unjust and tyrannical military regimes or to prop them up in the hope of preserving order

36

and repelling Marxist advance. This situation has inspired a new theology—liberation theology. The primary purpose of this theology is to apply the gospel message as lived out by Jesus amongst the poor in the Palestine of his own day to the situation confronting the masses in Latin America and other poor countries today. Father Gustavo Gutierrez, the Peruvian priest, has summed up liberation theology in these words: 'The deep human impact and the social transformation that the gospel entails, is permanent and essential because it transcends the narrow limits of specific historic situations and goes to the very roots of human existence: the relationship with God in solidarity with other men. The gospel does not get its full political dimension from one or other political option, but from the very nucleus of its message. If this message is subversive it is because it takes on Israel's hope: the kingdom as the end of domination of man over man, it is a kingdom of contradiction to the established powers and on behalf of man.'

This analysis is rooted in the gospels, but liberation theology has also been deeply influenced by Marxism. As a result, there has been widespread conflict in Latin America between the left wing Catholic revolutionaries and the right wing Catholic authoritarians. Both sides waited anxiously to see on whose side the Pope would throw his weight. In fact, from his first sermon, delivered after a stopover in San Domingo on 25 January, through his address in Mexico City, then in his speech at Puebla on 28 January, and again in subsequent homilies, the Pope made every attempt to strike a balance between the extremes.

He insisted on the primarily spiritual nature of the gospel message, but was equally clear that it entailed social consequences. At Puebla the Pope started off his words with an invocation of the Holy Spirit which set a prophetic tone: 'Let yourselves be led by the Spirit, open yourselves to His inspiration and His impulse and let it be He and no other spirit that guides and strengthens you.' He went on to outline with charismatic force the real task of the Church: 'Your principal duty is to be teachers of the truth, not a human unrational truth, but the truth that comes from God, the truth that brings with it the principles of the authentic liberation of man.' At the centre of evangelization is Jesus Christ who 'constitutes its essential content'. It is from a 'solid Christology' that doctrinal and pastoral problems have to be resolved. The Holy Father went on to reject the idea of Jesus as a politician or as one involved in the class struggle—the idea of 'Christ as a political figure, a revolutionary, as the subversive man from Nazareth, does not tally with the Church's catechesis'. The mission of Christ, he declared, goes far deeper: 'It consists in complete salvation through a transforming, peacemaking, pardoning and reconciling love.'

There could hardly be a more forthright rejection of the secular foundations of liberation theology and its Marxist exaggerations. Yet authoritarian regimes could draw no comfort from this, for the Pope went on to champion human

The Pope visits Mexico, 1979

dignity and human rights, which he fearlessly defended, making it clear that the rights of man, if they have no secular foundation, spring from his very nature as seen through Christian revelation. The Church, he declared in a normative passage, 'does not need to have recourse to ideological systems in order to love, defend and collaborate in the liberation of man: at the centre of the message of which she is the depositary and herald, she finds inspiration for acting in favour of brotherhood, justice and peace against all forms of domination, slavery, discrimination, violence, attacks on religious liberty and aggression against man'.

So much also for the oppressive regimes of Latin America. 'Who can deny that today individual persons and civil powers violate basic rights of the human person with impunity?' asked the Pope. 'Rights, such as the right to be born, the right to life, the right to responsible procreation, to work, to peace, to freedom and social justice, the right to participate in the decisions that affect people and nations? And what can be said when we face the various forms of collective violence like discrimination against individuals and groups, the use of physical and psychological torture perpetrated against prisoners or political dissenters? The list grows when we turn to the instances of abduction of persons for political reasons and look at the acts of kidnapping for material gain which attack so dramatically family life and the social fabric. We cry out once more: respect man, he is the image of God; evangelize, so that this may become a reality so that the Lord may transform hearts and humanize the political and economic systems, with man's responsible commitment as the starting point.' The quotation is in fact part of a message from Pope John Paul to the United Nations on 2 December 1978, the thirtieth anniversary of the Declaration of Human Rights.

POLAND

The theme of human rights was taken up again and developed by the Pope during what must rank as the most extraordinary and moving of all his visits, his return to Poland in June 1979. The nine-day visit began on 2 June and was accompanied by manifestations of enthusiasm, joy and delight never before witnessed behind the Iron Curtain, nor possibly in front of it.

The Pope's visit and his reception by his own people represented a triumph of the human spirit over tyranny and oppression which probably had as much impact outside Poland as within it. The world realized that after thirty years of Communist repression and indoctrination the Church in Poland was stronger than ever. This triumph was symbolized by the hugh cross erected for the papal mass in Victory Square in Warsaw, with the Polish crown and eagle forming a magnificent if provocative frontal to the altar, set up within a few yards of the Communist Party headquarters.

The Pope's visit formed a skein with a number of strands. First of all it was a highly emotional homecoming, a welcome to the famous son who had made history by being elected to the highest spiritual office in the Christian world. Second, it was an act of recognition of the heroic role played by Poland in resisting for so many years the twin tyrannies of Nazism and Communism and of its centuries-old fidelity to the Holy See. Yet it was more than this: it constituted a recognition of man's inherent spirituality, his dignity and his inalienable human rights. Again and again the Pope presented Christ as the key to the understanding of both Polish and human history. As he declared in his homily at the mass in Victory Square: 'The Church brought Christ to Poland, and this points the way to understanding of the great and fundamental reality which is man. For man cannot finally be understood without Christ, or rather man cannot ultimately understand himself without Christ. He can understand neither who he is nor what his proper dignity is, nor his vocation and final destiny; he cannot understand any of this without Christ. That is why Christ cannot be excluded from human history anywhere in the world.'

At these last words applause started in the vast crowd and continued for several minutes as it spread in great waves across the quarter of a million-strong congregation. The applause continued for so long that the Pope had to drop the next sentence of his text, which declared: 'The exclusion of Christ from the history of man is an act against man.'

In Warsaw the Pope had laid the Christological foundation of his view of human rights. When he came to Auschwitz he spelt out his conclusions. I recall my own visit to that vile concentration camp which witnessed the death of probably 4 million Jews and many Christians as well. That was a decade ago, but my feelings of horror remain vivid to this day. Yet I do recall a sign of hope in one of the darkest recesses of that place of blackness, a room in which the victims of the gas chambers were lined up before execution. I noticed there a graffito on the wall; it was of Christ, but not as one would expect of Christ crucified but of *Christos Pantocrator*, of Christ in triumph, the Christ so beloved by the Orthodox world.

That act of faith found its fulfilment in the words of Pope John Paul uttered over thirty years later: 'If the great cry of Auschwitz, the shout of man who was tortured here, is to bear fruit for Europe and for the world, then correct conclusions must be drawn from the declaration of human rights. Can anyone on this earth be surprised that a pope who came from the archdiocese which contains this camp, started his first encyclical with the words *Redemptor Hominis*—and that he devoted it in full to the cause of man, the dignity of man, the threats facing man, the rights of man—those inalienable rights which can be trampled so easily by man? It is enough to dress him in another uniform, to equip the apparatus of violence with a means of destruction. It is enough to impose on him an ideology in which the rights of man are subordinated to the needs of the system . . . .'

Elsewhere during his visit the Pope made it clear that his vision of Europe was far broader than one confined to the EEC. As with General de Gaulle, so with the Pope; Europe stretches to the Urals. While his visit was to Poland, the Pope prayed its effects would reverberate amongst the other Slav peoples of Eastern Europe. At Gniezno, where the shrine of St Adelbert is situated, the Pope hailed the saint as the apostle of all the Slavs. In a direct appeal to the neighbouring Slavonic nations, he said: 'When we reached these historical foundations we could not fail to hear, apart from our own language, the other Slavonic and related tongues. These languages must be heard especially by the first Slav pope in the history of the Church. Perhaps that is why Christ has chosen him.'

It was at Gniezno, too, that the Pope exercised an ecumenical role, embracing not only the followers in his own Communion but those in the Orthodox Church as well. 'Is it not Christ's will, is it not the intention of the Holy Spirit, that this Polish pope, this Slav pope, should at this precise moment manifest the spiritual unity of Christian Europe?' He went on to declare: 'Although there are two great traditions, that of the west and that of the east, to which it is indebted, through both of them Christian Europe professes "one faith, one baptism, one God, and

Father of us all".' The ecumenical theme was returned to in a sermon preached at Czestochowa, the site of Poland's most venerable shrine of the Blessed Virgin.

While the Pope was uncompromising in his proclamation of the Christian view of man there was nothing in his speeches of a cold war character. He has no intention of launching some kind of new crusade against the Soviet Union. Pope John Paul is light years away from being a cold war warrior. His approach is well exemplified in the words used to address the Polish bishops. 'We are well aware that mankind is divided in many ways. We have also in mind—perhaps above all—ideological divisions inherent in the programmes of different systems. The search for solutions which would enable human societies to cope with the task confronting them and live in justice is perhaps the main sign of our times. Let us respect everything in every programme. And let us utilize mutual experience.'

The year after the Pope's visit, Poland experienced a revolution. In the summer and autumn of 1980 the wave of strikes and general unrest led to the recognition of the union Solidarity. The Pope has been careful not to intervene directly in Polish affairs but there is no doubt that he has already had a dramatic influence there. The papal visit increased the self-confidence of the people and played its part in their taking a more independent line towards the Soviet Union and its Polish satellite government.

On 10 June, the Pope's extraordinary visit, which had been watched on television screens throughout the world, came to an end when he left Cracow airport for Rome. During his visit, he had demonstrated as never before, the strength of his character, the integration of his outlook and his profound appeal. In particular he established a rapport with young people in the crowds. At Gniezno he was seen singing with a crowd of 40,000 for more than ninety minutes. The visit constituted a unique confrontation between spiritual force and material power. Had the Pope been merely a local man he could well have been disposed of in a concentration camp or a mental hospital, but his international position protected him from such a fate.

He exploited his freedom to the full and gave new hope not only to his fellow countrymen but to millions throughout the world living under oppressive tyrannies. Let the last words of the visit be the Pope's own. They were uttered at Rome airport on his return from his homeland: 'I thank God that I was allowed to see Poland again, that blessed and fertile land in which I sank my roots as a man, a priest, and as bishop. . . . and now I thank God that he has permitted me to return to Rome, where my spirit each day ever more desires to identify itself and unite with the universal mission which has been entrusted to me. One fatherland, my homeland, has prepared me and gives me to a greater one, which is the more universal one, which, like my service, covers the whole world.'

Papal visit to Ireland, 1979

Opposite: The Pope returns to his native Poland, 1979

Pope John Paul's Ten Journeys

Pope John Paul's three-day visit to Ireland, which started on 29 September 1979, was like that to Poland, an act of recognition by the Holy See of the fidelity to Rome displayed in such an extraordinary fashion over the centuries by the Irish nation. From the moment the Holy Father stepped out of his Aer Lingus jet at Dublin airport and stooped to kiss the ground of Ireland, in what was becoming one of his hallmark gestures, his visit to what Cardinal Newman always referred to as 'our beloved sister island' was followed with the closest attention throughout Britain on television.

Again, this visit, like that to Poland, was characterized by deep emotion. There was joy, exuberance, delight, at times creating as much a carnival as a triumph. The people of Ireland responded massively to the visit. Probably more than half of the population participated in one or other of the religious or secular functions. One and a half million people, one-fifth of the population, attended the papal mass in Phoenix Park. At Galway, the mass for youth evoked extraordinary scenes of devotion to the Pope. The racetrack was packed with young people, cheering, waving flags and singing: 'He's got the whole world in his hands'. On the same day the Pope went on to Knock to indulge his passion for visiting spots associated with the Virgin Mary. Whether the Lady appeared or not in the last century at Knock, a near miracle certainly attended the papal visit in this one. Despite waiting for hours in the damp Irish climate, the nuns, priests and young people gave the Pope one of his most enthusiastic welcomes, and they were still dancing and singing long after the papal helicopter had soared into the sky.

Various themes were pursued by the Pope in his sermons and addresses on this occasion. He dealt with Irish history and its close connection with Rome; he praised the Irish people for their resistance to modern materialism and their fidelity to their faith. At Maynooth he recalled the priests to the greatness of their vocation; at Limerick in a farewell address he extolled the importance of the family. 'I want to say a very special word to all Irish parents,' the Pope said, 'marriage must include openness to the gift of children. Generous openness to accept children from God as the gift of their love, is the mark of the Christian couple. Respect the God-given cycle of life, for this respect is part of our respect for God himself, who created male and female, who created them in his own image, reflecting his own lifegiving love in the pattern of their sexual being. And so I say to all, have an absolute and holy respect for the sacredness of human life from the first moment of its conception. Abortion, as the Vatican Council stated, is one of the "abominable crimes" [*Gaudium et Spes*, 51]. To attack unborn life at any moment from its conception is to undermine the whole moral order which is the true guardian of the wellbeing of man. The defence of the absolute inviolability of unborn life is part of the defence of human life and human dignity. May Ireland never weaken in her witness before Europe and for the whole world, to the dignity and sacredness of all human life from conception until death. . . .'

Despite the importance of these events and addresses, it was at Drogheda in County Louth that the most significant point in the papal visit was reached. Before a vast congregation of nearly a quarter of a million people, many of them from the North, the Pope made a passionate and moving plea for an end to violence. He left Ireland and the world in no doubt about his total rejection of violence and of its anti-Christian character. Christianity, he made it plain, must seek solutions to unjust social or international situations, but he went on: 'What Christianity does forbid is to seek solutions to these situations by the ways of hatred, by the murdering of defenceless people, by the methods of terrorism. Let me say more: Christianity understands and recognizes the noble and just struggle for justice; but Christianity is decisively opposed to fomenting hatred and to promoting and provoking violence or struggle for the sake of "struggle". The command, "Thou shalt not kill", must be binding on the conscience of humanity, if the terrible tragedy and destiny of Cain is not to be repeated.'

The Pope went on to quote the warning given by Jesus in the gospel: 'All who take the sword will perish by the sword' (Matthew 26:52). He followed this with a philosophic analysis of the wickedness of violence: 'I join my voice today to the voice of Paul VI and my other predecessors, to the voices of your religious leaders, to the voices of all men and women of reason and I proclaim with a conviction of my faith in Christ, and with an awareness of my mission, that violence is evil, that violence is unacceptable as a solution to problems, that violence is unworthy of man, violence is a lie, for it goes against the truth of our faith, the truth of our humanity. Violence destroys what it claims to defend: the dignity, the life, the freedom of human beings. Violence is a crime against humanity, for it destroys the very fabric of society. I pray with you that the moral sense and Christian conviction of Irish men and women may never become obscured and blunted by the lie of violence, that nobody may ever call murder by any other name than murder, that the spiral of violence may never be given the distinction of unavoidable logic or necessary retaliation.'

The Pope's speech reached its climax when he made a direct appeal to the IRA: 'Now I wish to speak to all men and women engaged in violence. I appeal to you, in language of passionate pleading, on my knees I beg you to turn away from the paths of violence and to return to the ways of peace. You may claim to seek justice. I, too, believe in justice and seek justice. But violence only delays the day of justice. Violence destroys the work of justice. Further violence in Ireland will only drag down to ruin the land you claim to love and the values you claim to cherish. In the name of God I beg you: return to Christ who died so that

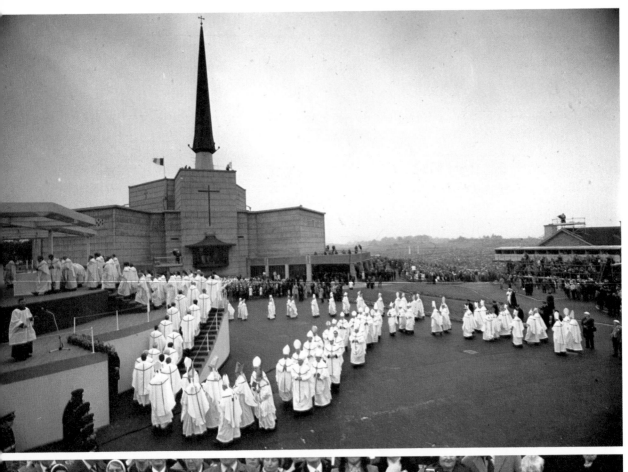

The Pope waves farewell to the Irish people, 1979

Opposite, above and below: The Pope visits the shrine of Our Lady
at Knock, Ireland 1979

men might live in forgiveness and peace. He is waiting for you, longing for each
one of you to come to Him so that He may say to each of you: Your sins are
forgiven; go in peace.'

The Pope did not confine himself to a condemnation of the men of violence
but concluded with a positive exhortation: 'Those who resort to violence always
claim that only violence brings about change. They claim that political action
cannot achieve justice, you politicians must prove them to be wrong. You must
show that peace achieves the work of justice, and violence does not. I urge you
who are called to the noble vocation of politics to have the courage to face up to
your responsibilities.'

I watched this address at home on the television and found it deeply moving. I
had long been concerned with the Irish question and some years ago was sent by
Mr Edward Heath, then Prime Minister, to Belfast to view the detention camp at

Long Kesh and to report back to him on the situation there. It gave me an encapsulated insight into the basic cause of the conflict. There in the prison camp behind the barbed wire were members of the indigenous population, dirty, dangerous, embittered, speaking with one kind of accent: and up at Stormont, which I went on to visit, representatives much more akin to Westminster politicians in their attire and appearance than anything I had come across in the valley below, speaking in quite different tones—representatives, in fact, of another race. From that time I never lost the conviction that the basis of the Northern Ireland problem was social rather than religious, that there were two races fighting for one piece of territory and that the most likely outcome was a fight to the death rather than an accord. On my return to London I made my report to Mr Heath and met him to discuss the whole situation. In my report I considered the possibility of doing away with Stormont but advocated caution—leaving abolition as a last resort. In the event Stormont was done away with.

Since then my pessimism about the whole Northern Ireland question had grown. Any intervention seemed inevitably to have been followed by denunciation from both sides. Eventually I had reached the rather craven conclusion that it was best to steer away from the whole matter. From this attitude of withdrawn complacency I was dramatically jerked by the Pope's address. I was then a member of the Cabinet, so I sat down and wrote to Mrs Thatcher, the Prime Minister, expressing my view that the Pope's visit had dramatically changed the situation in Ireland. I certainly did not believe that the IRA would respond to his appeal, and indeed they did not, but concluded that there was at least a good chance of separating the Catholic population in Northern Ireland from the terrorists. I added that in view of the Pope's closing words there was now a moral duty to respond politically to his appeal. The Prime Minister, who herself had been following the visit with close attention, seems to have reached similar conclusions. The result was a new initiative by the then Northern Ireland Secretary of State, Mr Humphrey Atkins, which he undertook doggedly but without total conviction, and which eventually petered out. It was a brave attempt to involve Catholics and Protestants in a new form of political power-sharing but it foundered on the old hatreds, enmities and jealousies.

There had been much discussion as to whether the Pope should visit Northern Ireland, and at one time it seemed likely that, despite the security problems, he would in fact do so. The assassination of Lord Mountbatten, shortly before the papal journey, tipped the scales against a Northern Ireland visit, and the Pope himself took the decision not to go there. The gathering at Drogheda was the closest he got to the North of Ireland.

On 1 October the Pope left Ireland for the United States, leaving behind him a self-image for the Irish people, closer to that of the island of saints and scholars than that of the holy gunmen. Perhaps this will be the most lasting effect of his visit. As Louis McRedmond wrote in the *Tablet* on 6 October 1979: 'I suspect that only we Irish understand the chord awoken so deep in our consciousness by the presence of the pastor of pastors. I spoke of history, that was at the heart of it. I do not mean history deliberately pondered. I mean an awareness, an awareness of identity and origin. You could not carry in your veins the blood of the generations who suffered degrading repression for the faith that was in them and remain unmoved. What the Irish knew last weekend, knew inchoately perhaps, was that the focal point of their forefathers' loyalty had come among them. Each man and woman and child voiced the soul stirrings of a people past as well as the excitement of their own experiencing. It was love in depth.'

THE UNITED STATES

The Pope's American visit started off on 1 October on Boston Common, where he addressed a gathering mainly of young people, in a manner which set the tone of much of what was to follow. It was as though the Pope was at pains to distance himself from the country which is the heart of what he thinks of as 'consumerism', a way of life which at times he appears to believe is as much a threat to human happiness and dignity as atheistic Marxism itself. The Pope of course has never lived in a capitalist society and is clearly repelled both by its materialism and its permissiveness.

The critical note struck at Boston reverberated throughout the six-day visit. As he declared to the young people of Boston: 'Faced with problems and disappointments, many people will try to escape from their responsibilities: escape in selfishness, escape in sexual pleasure, escape in drugs, escape in violence, escape in indifference and cynical attitudes. But today, I propose to you the option of love, which is the opposite of escape. If you really accept that love from Christ, it will lead you to God. . . . real love is demanding. I would fail in my mission if I did not clearly tell you so. For it was Jesus—our Jesus himself—who said: "You are my friends if you do what I command you" [John 15:14]. Love demands effort and a personal commitment to the will of God. It means discipline and sacrifice, but it also means joy and human fulfilment.'

This challenge to young people was paralleled on the following day at the Yankee Stadium in New York by his call for social justice. 'The poor of the United States and of the world are your brothers and sisters in Christ,' said the Pope. 'You must never be content just to leave them the crumbs from the feast. You must take of your substance and not just of your abundance, in order to help them and you must treat them like guests at your family table.' He went on to apply this teaching to the relationship between the developed and under-developed world: 'We must find a simple way of living. For it is not right that the standard of living of the rich countries should seek to maintain itself by drawing off a great part of the reserves of energy and raw materials that are meant to serve the whole of humanity. For readiness to create a greater and more equitable solidarity between peoples is the first condition for peace.'

On 3 October in Philadelphia, at a mass in the Logan Circle, he made a forthright condemnation of the permissive society: 'Here, as in any other field, there can be no true freedom without respect for the truth regarding the nature of human sexuality and marriage. In today's society, we see so many disturbing tendencies and so much laxity regarding the Christian view on sexuality that all have one thing in common: recourse to the concept of freedom to justify any behaviour that is no longer consonant with the true moral order and the teaching of the Church. Moral norms do not militate against the freedom of the person or the couple; on the contrary they exist precisely for that freedom, since they are given to ensure the right use of freedom.'

It was in Philadelphia too, on the following day, that he restated in the most uncompromising terms the character of the priesthood. He emphasized first its permanence: 'Priesthood is for ever—*tu es sacerdos in aeternum*—we do not return the gift that is given. It cannot be that God who gave the impulse to say "Yes", now wishes to hear "No".' He went on to stress the importance of celibacy. The call of God, he said, through the Church continues to offer us 'a celibate ministry of love and service after the example of Our Lord Jesus Christ. God's call has indeed stirred us to the depths of our being. And after centuries of experience, the Church knows how deeply fitting it is that priests should give this concrete response in their lives to express the totality of the "yes" they have spoken to the Lord who calls them by name to his service.'

He then fired off a third salvo in favour of the traditional view of the priesthood by declaring that its limitation to men as opposed to women was in accord with the prophetic tradition. 'It should help us, too, to understand that the Church's traditional decision to call men to the priesthood and not to call women, is not a statement about human rights, nor an exclusion of women from holiness and mission in the Church. Rather this decision expresses the conviction of the Church about this particular dimension of the gift of priesthood by which God has chosen to shepherd his flock.'

In Chicago on 5 October, the Pope made the most forthright statement of a conservative theological position, covering a number of moral issues, of the whole visit. He was speaking to the American bishops and as in all his visits it was the episcopal address to which he evidently attached prime importance. He took as the basis of his address the joint pastoral letter issued by the bishops three years previously, entitled 'To Live in Christ Jesus', which restated traditional moral theological positions in uncompromising terms. Having reasserted that marriage was inherently indissoluble the Pope went on to issue a complete condemnation of the practice of contraception: 'In exalting the beauty of marriage you rightly spoke against both the ideology of contraception and contraceptive acts, as did the encyclical *Humanae Vitae*. And I myself, today, with the same conviction of Paul VI, ratify the teaching of this encyclical, which was put forth by my predecessor "by virtue of a mandate entrusted by us by Christ".'

The Pope then went on to approve the teaching of the bishops that homosexual activity as distinguished from homosexual orientation is always morally wrong. 'In the clarity of this truth you exemplified the real charity of Christ; you did not betray those people who, because of homosexuality, are confronted with difficult moral problems as would have happened if, in the name of understanding and compassion, or for any other reason, you had held out false hope to any brother or sister.' The Pope also commended the bishops' statement for its reaffirmation of the right to life and the inviolability of every human life, 'including the life of an unborn child'.

In this address to the bishops the Pope laid down clearly two further conservative statements on vital theological matters: the teaching mission of the Church and the role of ecumenism. He accepted that there is in the community of the faithful a real activity of the Holy Spirit enlightening their minds and leading to insights of faith. He immediately added an important qualification: 'But these insights of faith and this *sensus fidelium* are not independent of the *magisterium* of the Church, which is an instrument of the same Holy Spirit and is assisted by Him. It is only when the faithful have been nourished by the word of God, faithfully transmitted in its purity and integrity, that their own charisms are fully operative and fruitful.'

On ecumenism, while the Pope stated clearly that it was the will of Christ to work earnestly for unity with other Christians, he went on to exclude intercommunion: 'We must pray and study together, knowing, however, that intercommunion between divided Christians is not the answer to Christ's appeal for perfect unity. And with God's help we will continue to work humbly and resolutely to remove the real divisions that still exist, and thus restore that full unity in faith which is the condition for sharing in the Eucharist.'

The Pope then descended on the federal capital of Washington, where President Carter with good manners and a fine disregard for any constitutional difficulties that might have arisen from the separation of Church and State, and with an equally clear perception of the political advantages of being seen with a charismatic pope, received him with all honours at the White House. Times had certainly dramatically changed since the defeat of Al Smith in his Presidential bid in 1928, principally because of his Catholicism, and the narrow squeak his religion caused John Kennedy when he was seeking the Democratic nomination in 1960 and in the election which followed.

The Washington visit was most notable because it produced the first signs of real opposition from Catholics to the Pope's strong conservative stand. Addressing a group of women members of religious orders in the hideous so-called National Shrine of the Immaculate Conception on the campus of the Catholic University of America, he was confronted by a challenge from Sister Theresa Kane, head of the Leadership Conference of Women Religious.

Sister Kane had been deputed to give the welcoming address, and took the opportunity to tell the Pontiff of 'the excruciating suffering of countless women, particularly sisters and nuns, who felt the Church treated them as second-class citizens of the Kingdom of God'. Sister Kane made it clear that she thought that the way should be opened for the ordination of women priests.

It is doubtful whether the Pope appreciated the full implications of her remarks and he went ahead with his prepared speech, though it did by chance contain a passage relevant to Sister Kane's plea. He pointed out that Mary was not among the apostles at the last supper and that she had no official part in the activities of the early Church. A group of sisters then stood up in protest against this attitude towards women in the Church.

The Pope also took the opportunity to strike a blow in favour of traditional clerical dress. He recalled his speech to the International Union of Superiors General the previous year, and declared that: 'Consecration to God should be manifested in the permanent exterior sign of a simple and suitable garb. This is not only my personal conviction but also the desire of the Church, often expressed by so many of the faithful.' The Pope here was echoing a passage from his address to the clergy at Maynooth, where he maintained: 'People need signs and reminders of God in the secular city, which has few reminders of God left. Do not help the trend towards "taking God off the streets" by adopting secular modes of dress and behaviour yourselves.'

It was in Washington too, in a sermon delivered during a mass on the Mall, that the Pope made his most forthright defence of the right to life. 'I do not hesitate to proclaim before you and before the world that all human life—from the moment of conception and through all subsequent stages—is sacred, because human life is created in the image and likeness of God. Nothing surpasses the greatness or dignity of a human person. Human life is not just an idea or an abstraction; human life is the concrete reality of a being that lives, acts, that grows and develops; human life is a concrete reality of a being that is capable of love and of service to humanity. . . . Human life is precious because it is the gift of God whose love is infinite; and when God gives life, it is for ever. . . . And so, we will stand up every time that human life is threatened. When the sacredness of life before birth is attacked we will stand up and proclaim that no one ever has the authority to destroy unborn life.'

Having condemned abortion, the Pope went on to affirm the indissolubility of the marriage bond and the duty to look after the sick and the old: 'When the sick, the aged or the dying are abandoned in loneliness, we will stand up and proclaim that they are worthy of love, care and respect.'

In the course of his visit to the United States, the Pope called at five major cities—Boston, New York, Philadelphia, Chicago and Washington DC—as well as one town in the Midwest, Desmoines, and a small local farming community. Perhaps the highlight of his visit occurred on 2 October when he addressed the UN General Assembly at the invitation of Dr Kurt Waldheim. The theme of the Pope's address was that of human rights, and he emphasized not only the vital importance of respecting human life but the rights of every individual to liberty and dignity irrespective of their creed or colour. The Pope made it clear that he wished to address all mankind and not merely his own followers: 'I wish to, above all, send my greeting to all the men and women living on this planet, to every man, every woman, without any exception whatever. Every human being living on earth is a member of a civil society, of a nation, many of them represented here.' The Pope rejected the idea of political activity as an end in itself: 'In reality what justifies the existence of any political activity is service to man, concerned and responsible attention to the essential problems and duties of his earthly existence in its social dimension and significance, on which also the good of each person depends.'

Rejecting also the exclusive measurement of man's progress by that of science and technology, he stressed that the principal yardstick of progress should be that of the primacy given to spiritual values and the progress of moral life. Recalling the horrors of Auschwitz he declared: 'This infamous place is, unfortunately, only one of the many scattered over the continent of Europe. But the memory of even one should be a warning sign of the path of humanity today, in order that every kind of concentration camp anywhere on earth may once and for all be done away with.'

Throughout his address the Pope stressed the importance of human rights and enumerated some of those universally recognized: 'The right to life, liberty and security of person; the right to food, clothing, housing, sufficient health care and rest and leisure; the right to freedom of expression, education and culture; the right to freedom of thought, conscience and religion, and the right to manifest one's religion either individually or in community, in public or in private; the right to choose a state of life, to found a family and to enjoy all traditions necessary for family life; the right to property and work, to adequate working conditions and a just wage; the right of assembly and association; the right to freedom of movement, to internal and external migration; the right to nationality and residence; the right to political participation, the right to participate in the free choice of the political system of one's people.'

Man, said the Pope, was essentially a two-world-centred creature: 'Man lives at the same time both in the world of material values and in that of spiritual values. For the individual living and hoping man, his needs, freedom and relationships with others never concern one sphere of values alone, but belong to both. Material and spiritual realities may be viewed separately in order to understand better that in the concrete human being they are inseparable, and to see that any threat to human rights, whether in the field of material realities or in that of spiritual realities, is equally dangerous for peace, since in every instance it concerns man in his entirety.' He rejected the idea that the meaning of human life could be explained by material and economic factors: 'I mean to the demands of production, the market, consumption, the accumulation of riches or of the growing bureaucracy with which an attempt is made to regulate these very processes. Is this not the result of having subordinated man to one single conception and sphere of values?'

It was when the Pope spoke of the danger of war that, like his predecessor, Paul VI, he became most compelling. Indeed he quoted directly from Pope Paul's warning issued from the same podium over a decade ago. The Pope's greatest urgency was displayed in his warnings about the effect of the arms race: 'The continual preparations for war demonstrated by production of ever more numerous, powerful and sophisticated weapons in various countries show that there is a desire to be ready for war, and being ready means being able to start it; it also means taking the risk that some time, somewhere, someone can set in motion the terrible mechanism of general destruction.'

In a prophetic passage the Pope seemed to be foreseeing the fate that could befall mankind: 'The ancients said: *si vis pacem para bellum*, but can our age still really believe that the breathtaking spiral of armaments is at the service of world peace? In alleging the threat of a potential enemy, is it really not rather the intention to keep oneself a means of threat, in order to get the upper hand with the aid of one's own arsenal of destruction? Here too it is the human dimension of peace that tends to vanish in favour of every new possible form of imperialism. It must be our solemn wish here for our children, for the children of all nations on earth, that this point will never be reached. And for that reason I do not cease to pray to God each day so that in his mercy he may save us from so terrible a day.'

In the United States the papal visit had an electrifying effect on Catholics and non-Catholics alike. The television coverage was continuous and unprecedented and, as elsewhere, the people responded to the Pope's spiritual presence. But what were the effects of his particular messages, particularly on moral issues? There was no doubt a strong element of affirmation in the papal teaching, though to many it must have seemed a series of traditional prohibitions. According to Father Andrew Greeley, the American priest–sociologist, what American Catholics were saying to the Pope was this: 'John Paul II we love you! But when we think you are wrong we are not going to take you seriously as a teacher.' American Catholics have developed the capacity of combining loyalty to the Church with selective obedience to official pronouncements. It would be absurd, therefore, to look for change, for example in Catholic attitudes to birth control, in the United States as a result of the papal visit. The overwhelming majority of American Catholics approve of the use of contraception and their habits seem unlikely to alter. They will, however, as a result of the visit have a clear impression of the importance of the spiritual foundations of life, and the Pope's embodiment of the power of the spirit is likely to have some lasting effect.

TURKEY

At the end of November, the Pope rounded off his 1979 travel series with a visit to the somewhat unlikely country of Turkey. In contrast to his visits to other countries this one was shrouded in silence. No great crowds gathered to welcome him and the Pope was surrounded by security arrangements. In view of what was to happen later in St Peter's Square, such precautions were wise.

The Pope arrived in Ankara on 28 November and it was there, in the chapel of the Italian Embassy, that he paid a remarkable tribute to Islam. 'When I think of this spiritual patrimony and of the value which it has for man and for society, of its capacity to offer above all to the young a direction to their lives, to fill the void left by materialism, to give a sure foundation to the very social and juridical order I ask myself if it is not urgent, just as Christians and Muslims have entered a new period of their history, to recognize and develop the spiritual ties which unite us.'

The Pope pointed out that Muslims venerated Jesus as a prophet although they did not recognize him as God. Furthermore, they honour the Virgin Mary and invoke her at their devotions. He quoted from the Koran and made clear that, in his view, a monotheist faith provided a basis for proper human conduct. Faith in God was professed in common by the descendants of Abraham whether Christians, Muslims, or Jews, and it provided a secure foundation for observing the dignity, fraternity and liberty of man.

From Ankara, the Pope went on to Istanbul, the Constantinople of the early Church. There he visited the Ottoman palace of Topkapi before going on to the former basilica of Santa Sophia, turned into a mosque by the Muslims after they conquered Constantinople in the fifteenth century. Istanbul provided the scene for the major purpose of the papal visit, an encounter with the Ecumenical Patriarch of Constantinople, Dimitrios I. This was not the first visit of a pope to the Phanar, the headquarters of the patriarchate, as Pope Paul VI had been there in 1967. Dimitrios I was elected to his office in 1972 as the successor to the Patriarch Athenagoras. In some ways it was a surprising choice, since he was little known in the Orthodox world and his ecclesiastical experience was limited. The choice of the fifteen electors of the Holy Synod was, however, limited, since by Turkish law the names of candidates have to be submitted to the Turkish authorities, who are able to exercise a veto. They had early indicated that Archbishop Iakovos, the Greek Orthodox Archbishop of North and South America, was unacceptable since he was an American citizen; and the natural successor to Athenagoras, the Metropolitan Meliton, was also ruled out. So Dimitrios was chosen.

The Pope and the Patriarch participated in a joint liturgical celebration at the Phanar in the Patriarch's own church of St George. The service included a *Te Deum*, a joint recital of the Lord's Prayer and two addresses, one from the Patriarch speaking in Greek, and the other from the Pope in Latin. Pope John Paul was warmly applauded by the members of the Greek Orthodox Church present, some shouting out in Italian, '*Viva il Papa*', and others cheered him in Greek. That evening the Pope celebrated mass at the Catholic Cathedral of the Holy Spirit with the Patriarch Dimitrios present. An even more significant function took place on the following day when the Pope attended the mass celebrated by the Patriarch for the feast of St Andrew. This was the first visit of a pope to an Orthodox mass since the schism of 1054. The Pope's presence acknowledged the authenticity of the eucharistic celebration, although he was there as a witness and not as a participant, and the occasion was given an added symbolic significance since it was the feast of St Andrew, Patron of Constantinople and younger brother of St Peter. St Andrew is also the patron saint of the entire Orthodox Church.

The Pope himself, despite the lack of razzmatazz, considered the visit to Istanbul as probably the most significant act of his pontificate. During his meeting with the Ecumenical Patriarch at the Phanar on 29 November he was frank about his purposes: 'The visit I am making today is intended as an encounter in the apostolic faith we share, so that together we might journey towards the full unity which has been damaged by unfortunate historical circumstances, above all in the course of the second millennium. What else should we do but express our firm hope in God that a new era will soon begin? On that account, Your Holiness, I am happy to be here today to express the profound respect and the sense of fraternal solidarity felt by the Catholic Church for the Eastern Orthodox Churches.'

During the eucharist in St George's on the following day the Pope spoke of St Peter as 'a brother among brothers', who was the first to be responsible for 'watching over the union of all and ensuring the symphony of the holy Churches of God, in fidelity to the faith that was given to the saints once and for all'. He went on to express the hope that he and the Patriarch would soon pray together at the tomb of St Peter as a proof of their 'impatient desire for unity'. He further declared that the time had come to hasten attempts to achieve perfect fraternal reconciliation, and hoped that when the third millennium began 'it will find us standing side by side in perfect communion.' The true question, said the Pope, that we should be asking ourselves, is not whether we are able to establish full communion but whether we have the right to remain separated.

The Patriarch, in his address, expressed his support for eventual full communion and a sharing of the breaking of bread, adding: 'Our ultimate goal is not simply the unity of our two Churches but the union of all Christians in the one Lord and in participation in the same cup.' In a joint declaration, both the Pope and the Patriarch committed themselves to hastening the day when full communion would be re-established between their two Churches and announced the opening of a theological dialogue which had been in preparation for a number of years.

PAPAL VISITS, 1980

AFRICA

For the first five months of 1980 the Pope busied himself with Church affairs in the Vatican, but at the beginning of May he was on the move again, this time for a ten-day visit to Africa, where he arrived on 2 May. In Africa, the Pope visited six different countries: Zaire, the Congo, Ghana, the Ivory Coast, Kenya and Upper Volta. During the visit he delivered more than seventy addresses and sermons, speaking in French. Once again these were all his own compositions. His longest visit was to Zaire, with nearly 50 per cent of its population Catholic. Other countries were not so favoured, but even when brief the visits were marked by exhilaration, boisterousness and delight.

In 1969 when his predecessor Pope Paul had visited Africa, he made a plea at Kampala for the Africanization of the Church. Pope John Paul assessed the consequences. While sharing Pope Paul's sentiments, he seemed at times more concerned to place limits to Africanization rather than to advance it further. Thus, in his address to the bishops of Zaire on the subject of evangelization, he declared that one aspect of this was the 'in-culturation' of the gospel, the 'Africanization of the Church', but then sounded a note of caution: 'Africanization covers wide and profound areas which have not yet been sufficiently explored, whether it is a question of the language in which to present the Christian message in such a way as to touch the minds and hearts of the Zaireans, of catechesis, of theological reflection, of the form of expression most suitable for the liturgy of sacred art or of the forms of Christian community life.'

Cardinal Joseph Malula, the Archbishop of Kinshasa, expressed regret that the Pope had not taken part in the Zairean liturgy, but too much need not be made of this, as Vatican officials explained. The Pope did not speak the language and felt that an attempt to participate in such a liturgy would be more artificial than real. Visually, this was a loss, since the celebrating priest while wearing normal vestments often adds a native head-dress and is accompanied to the altar by dancing acolytes carrying spears. One can see the Pope's point!

Pope John Paul showed his appreciation of African culture during his visit to the Ghanaian President, Dr Willa Limann, on 8 May. He assured the President that he fully understood that Africa had something special to offer to the world: 'One of the particular aspects of this continent is its diversity—but this is a diversity which is preserved intact by the undeniable unity of its culture: a conception of the world in which the sacred occupies a central position; a profound awareness of the link that exists between nature and the Creator; great respect for every form of life; a sense of family and community which flowers into open and joyful acceptance and hospitality; reverence for dialogue as a means of resolving differences and sharing points of view; spontaneity and *joie de vivre* expressed in the language of poetry, song and dance.'

The Pope, nevertheless, made it clear that Africanization did not mean adoption into the Christian ethic of polygamy and related customs, stressing in a number of his addresses the sanctity of marriage and family life based on monogamy. Thus at Kinshasa on 3 May, after he had extolled the ideal of monogamy, he summed up his position in these words: 'Used judiciously, African traditions can have their place in the building of Christian homes in Africa—I am thinking in particular of all the positive values related to the sense of family which are so rooted in the African soul and assume many aspects, all of them capable of prompting the reflection of the so-called advanced civilizations. . . . surely the most delicate problem is to take up this family dynamism, which is the legacy of the customs of the past, while at the same time transforming it and sublimating it within the perspectives of the society which is coming to birth in Africa.' The Pope was also in no doubt that celibacy for the clergy should be applied in the African context.

I do not wish to give the impression that the Pope's visit to Africa was joyless; it was not. On the fourth day of his pilgrimage something dramatic did happen, at Kisangani, a city in the midst of Zaire's densest jungle. The papal plane was greeted by a band playing religious tunes on horns, drums and guitars; lines of teenage girls in green swayed, sang and clapped their hands; everyone, including the press, began to dance including the staid diplomatic correspondent of Italy's *Corriere della Sera*. When the Pope reached the twin green lines of dancing girls he suddenly began to dance as well, his body swaying back and forth to the rhythm, a happy smile on his face. This was evidently one way of incorporating African dance into the liturgy of the Church! When the Pope left Africa from Abidjan airport, he once again warned against the extremes of

Arrival of the Pope on African soil, 1980

conservatism and innovation but the really important thing he told his African audience was to 'be yourselves'.

FRANCE

I was fortunate to be able to intercept the Pope between Africa and France for a private audience in Rome towards the end of May. The Pope, who left Africa for Rome on 12 May, was off again to Paris a week later on 30 May. The official reason for his visit to Paris was to address UNESCO, but in fact he managed to pack in a varied and full itinerary during his four days in France. Four major public masses were said, the first outside Notre-Dame on the Friday; the second at St-Denis, for the workers, on the Saturday; a third at Le Bourget airport on Sunday, where the Pope concelebrated with all the French bishops and another 1,000 priests in appalling weather; and finally a fourth outside the basilica of St Theresa at Lisieux, where he made a special pilgrimage to honour the Carmelite saint. There was a meeting with intellectuals at breakfast, and an official reception for 3,000 'personalities' at the Elysée Palace given by President Giscard, at which Georges Marchais, the Secretary of the French Communist Party, was observed presenting his wife to the Pope. Pope John Paul was received in France both as head of Church and head of State, being given a joint welcome from the President of the Republic, the Prime Minister and the Cardinal Archbishop of Paris. He inspected a guard of honour, but was spared the rigours of a state banquet.

The Pope had been well briefed on the problems of the French Church. He knew about the fall in figures of baptism, the low church attendance, the decline of Christian marriage and the shortage of vocations. His criticisms were directed even-handedly to the reformers amongst French Catholics who want to relax the traditional prohibitions on divorce, birth control and priestly marriage, and the traditionalists who will have no truck with the liberalizing measures of the Second Vatican Council. He accused the reformers of wanting to change the basis of Christian ethics in order to match modern morals, while the traditionalists were arraigned for shutting themselves up rigidly in ancient Church history and refusing to accept that God was working through the Vatican to update Catholic practice.

The Pope's references to France as the eldest daughter of the Church raised some smiles as well as eyebrows. The image is one favoured principally by the Catholic Right, although it dates from the conversion of King Clovis to Christianity in the fifth century. One surprise was his unequivocal support for the worker-priest movement in his address after the mass outside Notre-Dame. In striking contrast with the condemnation and hesitations long expressed by his predecessors at the Vatican, he gave the movement an unconditional *imprimatur*. 'Many French priests', said the Pope, '—and this has been particularly striking over the past thirty-five years—have been filled with a yearning to proclaim the gospel in the midst of the world, at the very heart of the life of our contemporaries, in every milieu, whether it be that of the intellectuals, the world of work, or the "fourth world", as well as to those who are far from the Church. To this end, they have employed new approaches of every kind and ingenious and courageous initiatives, going even so far, in the context of their mission to share the work and living conditions of the workers. . . . this pastoral concern conceived and carried out in union with your bishops is to your credit: may it continue through a ceaseless process of purification; this is the wish of the Pope.'

At the same time Pope John Paul took the opportunity to remind his listeners of the importance of celibacy as a sign of a priest's commitment. At St-Denis, he developed in his sermon a Christian view of work and the dignity it conferred upon man. He stressed the need to make production the instrument of man and not to arrange things the other way around. (It was perhaps unfortunate that the three points of his sermon, 'work, family and nation', recalled the motto of the Vichy regime rather than the revolutionary slogan of 1789 'liberty, equality and fraternity'. The Pope was careful to put matters right the following day at Le Bourget when he stressed that these ideas of the revolution were in essence Christian ones.)

At UNESCO the Pope made another appeal to world leaders to 'save the family of man from the horrible perspective of nuclear war', and coupled this with an analysis of the close links between religion in general, Christianity in particular, and culture. 'I am the son of a nation', said the Pope, 'whose neighbours have several times condemned it to death but which has survived and remained itself, preserving its identity despite partitions and foreign occupation by falling back on the resources not of its physical strength but of its culture.' As his addresses in France showed, the Pope has a clear historical image of Christian France, but he is aware also of the gap between the ideal and reality. Perhaps his presentation to the French nation of their Christian heritage will help to bridge this gulf.

BRAZIL

At the end of June the Pope set off on one of his most taxing journeys, the twelve-day, 17,500-mile tour of Brazil, during which he delivered nearly fifty addresses in the Portuguese he had learned especially for the occasion. Brazil is a country of 120 million people, 90 per cent of whom are Catholic, and the largest Roman Catholic country in the world. It also has the smallest percentage of practising Catholics—about 2 per cent of the 100 million who are baptized. A

Mass at Le Bourget
airport, France 1980

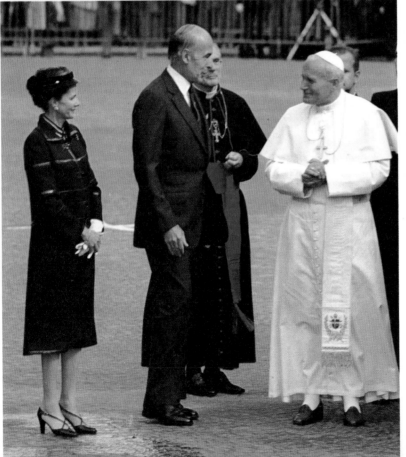

Pope John Paul II with
President Giscard d'Estaing,
France 1980

Papal visit to Brazil, 1980

Dramatic setting for a papal mass, Brazil 1980

country of variations and contrasts, both economically and geographically, the terrain ranges from deserts to jungles, the climate from the bitterly cold to the tropical. Brazil has great rural areas and huge cities made up of contrasting slums and skyscrapers, inhuman conglomerations, of which a good example is São Paulo, to which 20 per cent of Brazil's population has moved. Cardinal Evristo Arns, the Archbishop and one of the leading liberal clerics in the Church, struggles with nightmare social problems.

The Church has long been in conflict with the military regime. Four hundred of its members, including nine bishops, have been arrested, thirty-four priests have been tortured and eight killed over the past ten years, another ten have been kidnapped. On the other hand, some bishops have backed the government because of its anti-Communist stance but the overwhelming majority of priests and thoughtful lay people have joined in the struggle for justice and peace.

The Pope had held an early consultation with the Brazilian bishops in Rome and received divided advice, but once in Brazil he threw his weight on the side of social reform. When he met the Archbishop of Recife, Dom Helder Camara, the Pope, in a symbolic gesture, embraced him, despite his reputation as a clerical Red. The Pope supported the right to strike; he backed land reform, at Manaus on 10 July; he championed the rights of the Indians. Addressing the President of the Republic and other Brazilian leaders in the capital, Brasilia, on 30 June, the Pope declared: 'The Church preaches ceaselessly those reforms that are indispensable if the values without which no society worthy of the name can prosper are to be safeguarded and promoted, reforms aimed at a juster society, ever more conformed to the dignity of the human person. The Church encourages those who are responsible for the common good, especially those who are honoured to be called Christians, to undertake such reforms immediately, with determination and courage, prudently and effectively, relying on Christian criteria, objective justice and a genuine social ethic. To promote these reforms is one way of making sure that they are not sought instead under the impulse of schools of thought, by following which people would not hesitate to have recourse to violence and the suppression, direct or indirect, of the rights and fundamental liberties that are inseparable from the dignity of man.'

This theme of the necessity of reform to avoid violence was one that recurred in his speeches: 'Every society if it does not want to be destroyed from within must establish a just social order', he declared at Salvador. At São Paulo he addressed 150,000 cheering workers in the pouring rain. Brazil's most powerful union leader, Signor Ignacio Da Silva, hailed the Pope as a 'companion', which is the nearest one can get to calling a pope a 'comrade', and the Pope in return denounced an economic system 'which is concerned only with growth and profit'. He called on businessmen to pay higher wages and castigated conditions in the huge cities such as São Paulo as 'inhuman' and 'stunting'. The duty of employers was to provide employment. The Pope also visited Vidigal, one of Rio de Janeiro's hundreds of shanty-town slums. The authorities cleaned up the town for the occasion, providing Vidigal with piped water, some drainage and a new road. Furthermore, on the day of the Pope's visit, security men moved two-thirds of the 25,000 population out of the slums. Nevertheless, the Pope was able to get some idea of the degradation and poverty in which so many Brazilians live.

As in Mexico, the Pope insisted on the primacy of the spiritual over the political, and exhorted priests to keep out of politics. Nor would he allow the Brazilian bishops to ordain married men from the *'favelas'*, or shanty towns, despite their conviction that this was the only way of building up Christian communities in such settings. The Pope also disappointed some progressives by referring to the murder of Archbishop Romero of El Salvador, which had taken place in the spring, as a 'sacrilege' and not as a 'martyrdom'. Nevertheless the Pope's emphasis in favour of social reform was much more marked than in Mexico, where he seemed to have been more concerned to guard against the excesses of liberation theology.

GERMANY

More than three months elapsed after the Pope's return to Rome before his next visit abroad, that to Germany, the land of Luther and the Reformation. The Federal German Republic has a population of over 60 million, of which about half are Catholics, and a pope had not been present in Germany since Pius VI in 1782. Pope John Paul arrived at Cologne on 15 November to commemorate the septcentenary of St Albertus Magnus.

The visit had its difficulties. There was the psychological difficulty of a Polish pope visiting a country which had lost so much territory to Poland in the eastern frontier settlement after the Second World War. The weather in Germany in November is often bad, and on this occasion fully lived up to its reputation. Rain poured down on the 350,000 people gathered for an open-air mass in Cologne, and it continued wet and freezing cold for much of the visit. More serious had been the public controversy that had preceded the papal visit. The unfortunate St Albert Magnus was denounced as anti-semitic and anti-feminist—and he one of the Pope's favourite saints!

Another source of discord was the booklet published on behalf of the German bishops, one of three issued in preparation for the visit, which purported to be a brief history of the Church in Germany. In it Professor Baumer was less than charitable about Martin Luther, who was denounced as a man 'whose uncontrollable anger and polygamal spirit blinded him to Catholic truth'. As if this was not enough his marriage to a former nun was stigmatized as 'sacrilegious and

A damp arrival in Germany, 1980

Opposite above: Preaching in Cologne Cathedral, Germany 1980

Opposite below: Pope John Paul II with President Carstens, Germany 1980

stained by fornication'. Whatever the historical truth of these matters this was hardly tactful and the bishops had to retract hastily, but the damage had been done. A further complication was the letter from 130 theologians, including Professor Hans Küng, delivered to the papal nuncio in Bonn just before the arrival of the Pope. This asked six fundamental questions about the Church's commitment to the Third World, the arms race, ecumenism, admission of divorced people to Holy Communion, ordination of women and married men, and freedom of theological research.

In the event, the Pope triumphantly cleared all the obstacles and the visit to Germany proved a major success. At Cologne the Pope found the cathedral filled by university and other academic representatives and put the wretched St Albert firmly to rest in his historical context by stating that the content of his work was 'often time bound but his method of uniting faith and reason is still exemplary for us today'. At the official reception offered by President Carstens, he met a number of leading political figures including the Federal Chancellor, Helmut Schmidt, with whom he had private talks.

In public the Pope made affectionate references to Germany and praised German spiritual and cultural accomplishments. On Monday 17 November, he met leaders of the major Protestant Church in Germany, the Evangelical Church, for ecumenical discussions. The leaders were presented with a facsimile of Luther's translation of the Bible. More important, it was agreed to set up an ecumenical joint commission in the near future, to study in detail the questions which had been raised during the meeting, including inter-communion, ecumenical church services on Sundays as well as weekdays, and a project for a joint approach to marriage counselling in mixed marriages. The Pope particularly pleased the Protestants by his respectful references to the traduced Luther. He went on to draw on his own personal experiences in order to stress his commitment to ecumenism: 'You know that decades of my life have been affected by experience of the challenge of Christianity, of atheism and unbelief. Thus it is all the more evident to me what our commonly shared belief in Jesus Christ and in his words and work means in this world—as we are compelled by the need of the moment to overcome those differences which still divide the Churches and to affirm our growing unity.' The Pope also met the Chairman of the Central Council of German Jewry.

At Fulda on 17 November, the Pope addressed clergy and seminarians and took the opportunity to express once again the importance he attached to the celibacy of the Catholic priesthood. After praying at the tomb of St Boniface, he addressed the German Episcopal Conference, explaining that the three matters which were particularly close to his heart were worthy seminaries, sound theology and a supportive environment for the priest in his life of celibacy and devotion. In an address to the laity on the following day he reminded them that on theological questions they must be willing to 'accept the decision of those, who as pastors of the Church, are responsible for the protection of matters of faith'.

In the evening the Pope spoke to a meeting of German theologians, stressing three perspectives which he believed to be of great importance. First, the complexity of current theological studies and the danger that the aim of theology might be obscured. Second, the primacy of scripture as a basis of theological investigation; and third, the relationship between theology and faith, the former needing to serve the latter and not the other way round. The Pope said: 'The theologian teaches in the name of, and on behalf of the ecclesiastical community of the faith. He should and must make new suggestions which contribute to the understanding of faith, but these are only an offering to the whole Church, which must be corrected and expanded in brotherly discussion before the Church can accept it. At its profoundest, theology is a selfless service to the community of the faithful.'

The Pope's last day in Germany, 19 November, was marked by a mass for youth in the Theresienwiese, a park in Munich more famous for its October beer festival than its eucharistic celebrations. On this occasion the mass was dedicated to the theme of youth. The Pope made an appeal to the young men present to consider a vocation to the priesthood, and urged his listeners to reject the temptations of drugs, alcohol and other illicit sensual pleasures. After the mass, the Pope faced an incident similar to that in Washington. A young woman, Fräulein Barbara Engl, who had been chosen to address the Pope on behalf of the Munich Association of Catholic Youth, departed from her prepared text to point out that young people in Germany found it difficult to understand why the Church 'clings fearfully to traditions' and in particular priestly celibacy. She asked also why there could not be more participation by women in the life of the Church: 'Young people', she declared, 'have the feeling that the Church is more interested in perpetuating divisions with other Christians rather than stressing what brings us together. They find their concern for friendship, sexuality and partnership receives only negative answers.' The Pope listened to what she had to say with his head in his hands, but there was no response.

The German visit ended with a speech to a gathering of artists and a stressing by the Pope of the relationship between art and the Church, and after celebrating a mass for old people and the disabled in Munich Cathedral, he returned to Rome in the evening. As in France, the principal purpose of his visit seemed to have been to call back the German nation to its Christian foundations and roots.

Over page: The crowds gather at Fulda Cathedral, Germany 1980

PAPAL VISITS, 1981

So ended the 1980 series of papal visits, but early in the new year, the Pope set out on a new trajectory, making his first journey to Asia, the Philippines and Japan, stopping over briefly at Karachi to say mass and to chat with President Zia. The two countries chosen for the Asian sortie could hardly have been more contrasting. The Philippines, with its 49 million population, 85 per cent of whom are Catholics, provides Asia with its principal Christian community. In Japan, on the other hand, Christians are only a tiny proportion of the population and Catholics number a mere 0.5 per cent.

THE PHILIPPINES

Pope John Paul arrived in Manila on the morning of 17 February, where he was greeted personally by President Marcos. Fears had been expressed before the visit that the Pope would be taken over by the regime for its own ends. The repressive character of the Marcos government is well known, and indeed eight years of martial law ended only a few weeks before the Pope arrived.

Cardinal Sin, the splendidly named Archbishop of Manila, was determined that the visit should be a pastoral one without any political implications, a viewpoint shared by the Pope, who declared at the airport: 'I come to you in the name of Jesus Christ. And I come on a visit of a religious and pastoral nature to proclaim his gospel, to proclaim salvation in his name.'

The Pope gave substance to these words by going off at once for a meeting with Filipino members of female religious orders at the National Shrine of Our Lady of Perpetual Help. In the afternoon he was received by President Marcos and members of the Government. It was on this occasion that while stressing the pastoral nature of his visit, he made one of his strongest statements in defence of human rights. His hosts must have been somewhat abashed by these words: 'One can never justify any violation of the fundamental dignity of the human person or of the basic rights that safeguard this dignity. Legitimate concern for the security of a nation, as demanded by the common good, could lead to the temptation of subjugating to the state the human being and his or her dignity and rights. Any apparent conflict between the exigencies of security and of the citizens' basic rights must be resolved according to the fundamental principle—upheld always by the Church—that social organization exists only for the service of man and for the protection of his dignity, and that it cannot claim to serve the common good when human rights are not safeguarded.' Not content with this, the Pope concluded his remarks with a reminder to the ministers present to 'see enacted those reforms and policies that aim at bringing about a truly human society, where all men and women and children receive what is due to them, to live in dignity, where especially the poor and under-privileged are made the priority concern of all'.

Two other principal themes can be detected in the Pope's addresses. When he spoke to male members of religious orders in the cathedral at Manila on his first day, he warned them against excessive involvement in politics. He reminded them of what he had said at Puebla: 'You are priests and religious; you are not social or political leaders or officials of a temporal power. . . . let us not be under the illusion that we are serving the gospel if we dilute our charism through an exaggerated interest in the wide field of temporal problems.' The Pope was also at pains to condemn the resort to violence. Speaking at Tondo, a poor waterfront district of Manila, on 18 February, he warned: 'Do not be tempted by ideologies that preach only material values or purely temporal ideals, which separate political, social and economic development from the things of the spirit, and in which happiness is sought apart from Christ. The road towards your total liberation is not the way of violence, class struggle or hate; it is the way of love, peaceful solidarity.' At the same time the Pope exhorted those holding political power to be poor in spirit, and to remember that power is given for the common good alone. Those in power should never cease to devise means to organize all sectors of society according to the demands of the dignity and equality which constitute the birthright of all whom God has created.

JAPAN

The Pope arrived in Japan on Monday afternoon, 23 February, to be greeted by only 200 people, a sharp contrast to the great crowds which had awaited him in other countries. Quite apart from the dearth of Catholics, the airport is situated far from Tokyo and security is tight because of the violent demonstrations that have taken place against its construction in the past. Out of the total Japanese population of 117 million, there are only 400,000 Catholics.

The day after his arrival the Pope met the Emperor Hirohito, in a picturesque encounter that constituted the first meeting between a pope and a Japanese emperor. But it was on the following day at Hiroshima on 25 February, that he made his major contribution in a passionate appeal for peace. Speaking in nine languages, including Japanese and Chinese, the Pope recalled: 'On this very spot where, thirty-five years ago, the life of so many people was snuffed out in one fiery moment, I wish to appeal to the whole world on behalf of life, on behalf of humanity, on behalf of the future. To the heads of state and of government, to those who hold political and economic power, I say, 'Let us pledge ourselves to peace through justice, let us take a solemn decision—now —that war will never be tolerated or sought as a means of resolving differences.' The Pope went on to reflect on the moral impact of the dropping of the atomic bombs on Hiroshima and Nagasaki: 'The human mind had in fact made a terrible discovery. We realized, with horror, that nuclear energy would henceforth be available as a weapon of devastation; then we learned that this terrible weapon had in fact been used, for the first time, for military purposes. And then there arose the question that will never leave us again: will this weapon, perfected and multiplied beyond measure, be used tomorrow, and if so, would it not probably destroy the human family, its members and all the achievement of civilization?'

In speaking in this manner, the Pope was voicing a fear which seems to be constantly before his mind—that a nuclear holocaust could at any moment engulf humanity. He complemented his warning by a positive tribute to science and technology, which he hailed as 'a wonderful product of a God-given human creativity, since they have provided us with wonderful possibilities and we all greatly benefit from them'. But the note of anxiety immediately returned: 'Today I feel inspired to say this to you; surely the time has come for our society, and especially for the world of science, to realize that the future of humanity depends, as never before, on our collective moral choices.'

The Pope stressed that it is only through a conscious choice and through a deliberate policy that humanity can survive. Speaking with great urgency he declared: 'Our future on this planet, exposed as it is to nuclear annihilation, depends upon one single factor: humanity must make a moral about-face. At the present moment in history there must be a general mobilization of all men and women of goodwill. Humanity is being called upon to take a major step forward, a step forward in civilization and wisdom. A lack of civilization and ignorance of man's true values brings the risk that humanity will be destroyed. We must become wiser.' The Pope emphasized, as he had done in his address to UNESCO in Paris, that technical issues must be subjected to ethical judgements: 'I urge all scientists, centres of research and universities to study more deeply the ethical problems of the technological society, a subject which is already engaging the attention of a number of modern thinkers.'

From Hiroshima the Pope moved on to Nagasaki where he honoured the sixteenth-century Catholic martyrs, as well as the victims of the atomic attack of 1945. He met a number of the surviving victims, telling them: 'Your life here today is the most convincing appeal that could be addressed to all people of goodwill—the most convincing appeal against war and for peace. . . . we are all indebted to you for the living and constant appeal for peace that you are.' The Pope left Japan on 26 February, returning to Rome via Anchorage in Alaska.

Pope John Paul's Ten Journeys

THE FUTURE OF PAPAL TRAVEL

When the Pope returned to Rome in February 1981 a number of further travel projects had already been arranged, including visits to Switzerland, Lourdes and Britain. But doubts were thrown on the future of these and other plans by the attempt on his life on 13 May in St Peter's Square by the Turkish fanatic Mehmet Ali Agca. This twenty-two-year-old terrorist had travelled to Italy some weeks before to prepare for his grisly mission, which was inspired by a mixture of political and religious motives. Unlike so many contemporary attempts and acts of assassination, it was not one of pathological exhibitionism but was ideologically motivated. The Holy Father was struck by four bullets, two hitting his right arm, one his left hand, and the fourth passing right through his body. He collapsed into the arms of his Polish secretary, Fr Stanislaw Dziwisz, and was rushed to the Gemelli hospital where a four-and-a-half-hour operation took place. The world watched in shock and horror as the Pope struggled for his life: at one time he was in real danger of death but his strong constitution and will pulled him through. In his absence Cardinal Casaroli presided over the affairs of the Church.

The Swiss and Lourdes visits were cancelled, but the planned trip to Britain was allowed to go ahead. Visits to Spain and Switzerland seem likely to be arranged. Although the Pope has made an excellent recovery from the shooting, it seems likely that the number of papal journeys in the future and their scope are likely to be scaled down. One development could be that the itineraries will be less intensive, with fewer massive public events and greater use of the resources of broadcasting and television to publicize his visits.

There is a further point: the Pope is known not only to have sustained physical injury but to have been psychologically affected as well. A man with a strong belief in the constant manifestation of God's providence and will through signs and events, he has entered a period of self-questioning as to whether the policy he has followed, in which he has exposed himself to large crowds, is in accordance with the divine will. No doubt the Pope will eventually cease to be introspective about the matter but he is certainly reviewing his future plans in the light of the near tragic events in St Peter's Square.

A change in the style of papal travel might well be desirable on quite other grounds. If papal visits could be made less dramatic and public it would give the opportunity for a more profound and detailed exchange of views than the present style allows. For many, this would be a welcome development.

CHINA AND THE VATICAN

There is no doubt that the Pope will visit other countries—Spain and Switzerland are high on his list—but it looks as though the land which most attracts him now is China. It is a country which presents a particularly difficult problem as there are two groups of Catholics—those loyal to Rome and those who have founded a Chinese National Church closely linked to the Communist regime. When I visited China in 1978, I was particularly interested in the state of the Church there and was able to visit the Catholic cathedral in Peking as well as a Protestant chapel. I held conversations with the parish priest—a member of the Chinese National Church, which broke off its relations with Rome after the revolution. The cathedral is a strange anachronism with its nineteenth-century French Gothic style and its regular celebration of the Latin Tridentine mass. Its services are badly attended but it is difficult to draw clear conclusions from this. Many Catholics no doubt stay away through fear and others out of loyalty to Rome. Before the Communist revolution there were probably about 3 million Catholics in China, some of them in the great cities like Shanghai, Canton and Peking.

While in Peking, I raised with my hosts the question of opening diplomatic relations with the Vatican but the suggestion evoked little interest. It was pointed out to me that it would be impossible for such a development to take place while the Vatican continued to recognize Taiwan. In Rome the following October, I discussed my visit with Monsignor Casaroli—then one of the deputies to Cardinal Villot, papal Secretary of State, and he expressed great interest in the Chinese situation. Undoubtedly, there are those in the Vatican who realize the importance of China to the Church as one of the fastest rising powers in the world today.

China and the Vatican have been at arm's length for a considerable time but there are now signs of a thaw. Taiwan undoubtedly presents a formidable obstacle. The Vatican has not in the past broken off diplomatic relations with other states, although they are sometimes allowed to wither away. There are, however, significant arguments against breaking with Taiwan, where the Roman Catholic Church is 200,000 strong with a flourishing system of schools and even a university.

The Catholic Church's interest in China goes back to the late sixteenth century. At that time the Jesuits were welcomed in Peking and their leader Father Matteo Ricci, was anxious to integrate Chinese and Catholic culture. This initiative was eventually rejected by Rome in 1704, in what Peter Nichols in his informative account of the Church in China has rightly described as one of the 'historic errors committed by the Church'. Had another policy been followed, China might possibly have become a Christian country. That dream faded and

Roman Catholics remained a minority in China, sometimes accepted, sometimes persecuted, always tenacious in their faith. A break came in 1949 when the National Association of Patriotic Catholics was set up by the regime and relations with Rome became strained. The Association elected its own bishops, Mao Tse-tung became implacably hostile, and in 1958 a condemnation was issued by Pius XII from Rome. All bishops and priests who had remained loyal to the Holy See were either imprisoned or sent into exile.

The Bishop of Peking, Wang Sitin, died in late 1978 and in July 1979, Peking announced the election and consecration of a bishop, Michael Fu Tieh-shan to the See of Peking. Rome would hardly have approved of this but in August of the same year the Pope made an unprecedented reference to China and expressed his appreciation of the respect being shown to religion there. He expressed the wish that there would be new opportunities for direct contact with Chinese Catholics. In the same year a Chinese Jesuit, Father Michael Choo, was allowed to return to the mainland after an interval of thirty years. There are probably over 100 Chinese Jesuits in China, although the whereabouts of many of them are unknown. Other signs of the thaw have been the visits of Cardinal Etchegaray of Marseilles and Dr Hans Küng to Peking. In March 1980 the Archbishop of Vienna, Cardinal König, made a ten-day visit to China to explore how relations with the Peking regime might be improved. The Cardinal is the head of the Secretariat for relations with non-believers.

The Pope takes a personal interest in China, and the Vatican is prepared to be flexible over the problems separating the Church and the Chinese Republic. There might well be a willingness to downgrade the diplomatic relations between Taiwan and Rome. The Vatican has in fact declined to appoint a full nuncio to Taiwan, where it is represented by a minor official. When Pope John Paul was in Manila he received a group of 100 Chinese Christians. Addressing them, he said: 'Whatever difficulties there may have been, they belong to the past, and now it is the future we have to look to. . . . I am convinced that every Catholic within your frontiers will fully contribute to the building up of China since a genuine and faithful Christian is also a faithful and genuine citizen.' He pointed out that the Church in China was seeking no privileges, only that 'all those who follow Christ may be able to express their faith freely and publicly and live according to their consciences'. The reaction of the Bishop of Peking was guarded, but he was not totally hostile to the Pope's words.

In September 1980 a veteran Chinese Jesuit, Monsignor Dominic Tang was released from jail after twenty-two years of imprisonment, in what looks like a promising thaw in Vatican–Chinese relations. In June 1981 he was appointed Archbishop of Canton by the Vatican, but the reconciliation was short-lived. The Association of Peking Catholics criticized the appointment as it was denounced by the Peking government as an illegal interference in Church internal affairs.

Undoubtedly the changing relationship between China and the Vatican is one of the most intriguing contemporary developments in Church–State relations, which could be of immense significance for the future.

WORKING FOR PEACE

The Holy Father might wish to pay a visit to the United Nations in the cause of preserving world peace. On 12 December 1981 the Vatican announced that apostolic delegations were to be sent to Washington, Paris, London and the United Nations to outline the 'terrifying prospects' of the use of nuclear weapons. The purpose of the delegations is to present the conclusions of a study by the Pontifical Academy of Sciences, which the Pope had ordered to be carried out on 'the prospects connected with the use of nuclear arms, with particular attention to the disastrous effects of an atomic war'. The Pope regards the campaign for nuclear disarmament as one of the major themes of his pontificate. His fears are growing of a nuclear holocaust, and further initiatives are likely to be taken in the future.

4

The Calling of the Man
from a Far Country

On the evening of Saturday 6 August 1978, the feast of the Transfiguration, Pope Paul VI slipped quietly and peacefully into the next world. He was in his eighty-first year and lay down his burdens with relief. For some time he had suffered from arthritis, and depression plagued him as he grew older. Death, when it called, came not so much as an enemy as a friend. The dead pope was laid out in state at Castel Gandolfo, the popes' summer residence, where he had died. There were no scenes such as those which marred the death of Pius XII in the same place. Then, it will be recalled, the dying Pontiff was cared for by Dr Galeazzi Lisi, the eccentric and publicity-conscious physician who had gained the Pope's confidence in his latter years. It was he who arranged to raise the window curtain as a signal to a waiting journalist that the Pope was dead. As it turned out, the curtain was moved prematurely by a nun so that reports of the death of Pius XII appeared in the Roman papers while the Pontiff was still alive. As if this was not enough the doctor's eccentric embalming process proved inadequate so that the body was decomposing even as it lay in state at St Peter's. Oddly enough the body of Paul VI was not embalmed either, but this was by his express instructions and intended as a symbol of the acceptance of his mortality.

PAUL VI

When the Pope died, I could hardly have been further away from Rome—winging my way across the Pacific towards China. On my arrival at Hong Kong on 7 August, the first thing I noted was that the flags were at half-mast. The explanation came swiftly when the government official greeting me offered me his condolences with the news that the Pope was dead. So, I reflected, that great and good man was gone: the pope sensitive to the need for change and at the same time conscious of his duty to preserve and pass on the prerogatives of his office; the pope whose controversial encyclical *Humanae Vitae*, condemning artificial contraception, had stirred up a hornets' nest which plagued him in his last years. Contemporaries, taking their cue from Pope John, looked upon him as 'Amletico' (Hamlet-like), but I venture to think that judgement inadequate. Pope Paul was a man of skill, insight and compassion, aware of the complexities of the problems facing the Church, and concerned to reconcile the prestige of the papacy with the changes introduced by the Vatican Council. He brought the Council to a successful conclusion, kept the Church together, modernized the liturgy, and embarked upon the beginnings of synodical government, though he was not destined to bring these to their conclusion. He was open and concerned about the problems of the Third World and confirmed the ecumenical break-through made by his predecessor Pope John. By any standards this is a remarkable record.

During his last years I shared the general disillusion with his reign. Looking back now from a different standpoint I am able to recognize him as one of the great popes of the century. I recall my last meeting with him some years ago, just as the shadows were beginning to lengthen. His final words to me had a prophetic ring. 'Remain faithful,' he said, and then again, 'remain faithful,' and then again, a third time he repeated the exhortation. It was like the opening bars of the overture to Verdi's opera *La Forza del Destino*. The next and the last I saw of him was the simple wooden coffin that contained his remains, lying by his express command not on a catafalque but on the steps of St Peter's.

THE FIRST CONCLAVE

By the time of the conclave to elect his successor, in late August, I was back in Europe, and arrived in Rome on 24 August, the day before it opened. I was in St Peter's for the mass concelebrated by the cardinals seeking the guidance of the Holy Spirit on their deliberations. Cardinal Villot, the papal Secretary of State, presided, and it proved an occasion on which one was able to identify the outstanding cardinals of the conclave. I was able to pick out Cardinals Wyszynski, Willebrands and Suenens, amongst others. Cardinal Hume had kindly invited me to lunch with him at the English College after the mass, and we had a happy interval together gossiping and taking 'snaps' before he was whisked off in the late afternoon, carrying his *Middlemarch* into the conclave. I suggested to him that he might not be coming back and he countered with the enigmatic remark: 'I would not be the sort of pope that you would want.' As my main concern was for the election of an open-minded and liberal pope I did not fully understand the point of this sibylline utterance.

Many were not praying to the Holy Spirit, and without his aid were laying down exactly the sort of pope whom they wanted to see. Notable amongst them was the American priest–sociologist Father Andrew Greeley, who issued the following job description for the new pontiff: 'At the present critical time of its history, faced with the most acute crisis, perhaps since the Reformation, and dealing with the world in which both faith and community are desperately sought, the papacy requires a man of holiness, a man of hope, a man of joy. A sociologically orientated job description of the pope, in other words, must conclude that the Catholic Church needs as its leader a holy man who can smile.' A rather more demanding set of requirements was contained in an 'open letter' to the conclave signed by a number of theologians linked with the review *Concilium*. They demanded a pope open to the world, a guide in spiritual matters, a pastor of authenticity, committed to collegiality and to the ecumenical movement.

The conditions under which this paragon was to emerge had been laid down in advance by the late Pope in his apostolic constitution *Romano Pontifici Eligendo*. The constitution enjoined secrecy on all taking part in the conclave and laid down heavy penalties for any breach of confidentiality. Cardinals aged over eighty were excluded from the conclave, much to their chagrin. Preparations were in the joint hands of Cardinal Confalonieri, the Dean of the College, who at the age of eighty-five was himself excluded from the voting, and Cardinal Villot, who was young enough to qualify.

I had never attended a papal conclave before and was fascinated and amused by everything, from the rusty iron stove with its chimney poking through the ceiling of the Sistine Chapel, the machinery by which the world would learn of the election of the new pope, to the makeshift arrangements to accommodate all the cardinals in rooms ranging from magnificence to dingy cubby holes.

The atmosphere in Rome was a cross between a religious *festa* and a major sporting event. At 4.30 p.m. on the Friday the cardinals vanished into the Sistine Chapel singing the *Veni Creator Spiritus*. Monsignor Virgilio Noè pronounced the *extra omnes* and the participants were sealed up in the conclave. The next day, Saturday 26 August, I duly took up my position in the Piazza at noon and was rewarded by seeing the first papal smoke of my life belching out of the iron chimney. It was black and very satisfying as it dispersed against the clear blue Roman sky. I retired for luncheon and a siesta and was back in position at 5.30 on a perfect Roman evening to await events. At 6.30 what looked like white smoke started pouring out of the Sistine Chapel chimney and there were cries of 'blanco, blanco' from a group of agitated Spaniards near me. As they were jumping up and down, the black smoke turned to a dirty grey then into a shade of white, then into black again, and proceeded to go through all the shades of its restricted colour spectrum. For over half an hour the maddening smoke teasingly changed colours, going from white to grey to black and back again. So much for the new chemical processes which, we had been informed, were going to do away with the uncertainties of the past. Finally, just after seven, the smoke became definitely white and at the same time its colour was confirmed over Vatican Radio.

At just about 7.10 the great windows on the balcony in the centre of St Peter's opened and a few minutes later Cardinal Pericle Felici appeared and announced to the waiting multitude: *'Annuncio vobis gaudium magnum: habemus papam. . . . Albinum Luciani qui sibi imposuit nomen Ioannem Paulum Primum.'* The crowd swiftly realized that it was the Patriarch of Venice, Cardinal Luciani, who had carried off the prize, and they burst into applause. Then came the tiny white figure with the red cape, giving the blessing: *'Urbi et Orbi'* for the first time. The only two friends who had predicted the possibility of such an outcome were the British consul in Venice, and the British Minister to the Holy See. Yet there was a third who had given me a clear enough indication, Cardinal Suenens, the Archbishop of Brussels. I saw him the night before the conclave opened and he gave me *his* job description for the new pontiff: he should be 'a pastoral pope, a humble man who knows his limits and who will be collegial'. It was an identikit portrait of Papa Luciani.

THE ELECTION OF ALBINO LUCIANI

How did Albino Luciani 'make it' when other better-known or more favoured personalities dropped out of the running? Secrecy is meant to surround a papal conclave like a shroud, and Paul VI thought he had sewn the integuments more tightly together than ever before. In fact he had provided a loophole or keyhole of his own. The octogenarian cardinals, although excluded from the conclave, would naturally expect to hear what had gone on inside and they did, but they were bound by no vow of secrecy, and in the humiliating circumstances of their exclusion were not likely to be models of discretion. Here then was a ready source of information. Furthermore, journalist Vaticanologists are adept at picking up the slightest hint or clue, and some prelates were certainly not averse to providing such titbits. As a result, we can be reasonably sure of what actually went on inside the Sistine Chapel.

Before the conclave, the kind of pope that the cardinals (as opposed to the *Concilium* theologians) wanted was reasonably clear. They were looking for a 'pastoral pope', which, whatever was meant by that, excluded curial careerists and put paid to the chances of Cardinal Benelli. The majority did not want a reactionary and this disposed of Cardinal Siri, any more than they wished to elevate one of the great liberal reforming prelates of the north, and that put paid to the chances of Cardinal Suenens. What they did want was someone who would give strong and moderate leadership to the Church after the storms of the Council and the introversion and uncertainty of Paul VI's last years. As I wrote at the time, in the *Economist* of 2 September 1978: 'From the moment of Pope Paul's death a month ago, it was clear that most of the cardinals did not want a pontiff hungry for a change. They were looking for a moderate, open-minded conservative, and they have got one. After the upheavals of Pope John and the Second Vatican Council and the hesitations and agonies of Pope Paul, they were in no mood for radical reform. It is equally clear that they wanted a pastoral, not a diplomatic, academic or administrative, pope. They were looking for a man of orthodoxy, safe on doctrinal essentials, but ready to travel on cautiously down the road opened up by the Vatican Council. So Cardinal Luciani became the majority's man.' Others, who had headed the forecasts, such as Cardinals Baggio, Bertoli and Pignedoli, were simply swept aside by the unknown from Venice.

There appear to have been three or four ballots, two at noon and another one or possibly two in the evening. On the first ballot, which was essentially a test vote for opinions and for 'favourite sons', Cardinal Luciani appears to have obtained a reasonable number of votes. On the second he obtained considerably more and it was clear from the relaxed atmosphere at luncheon that a new pope was beginning to emerge. This reconstruction of what happened is confirmed by the words of the Pope himself, the day after his election. Speaking from the balcony of St Peter's at noon, he commented, 'As soon as things became dangerous for me, two of my colleagues whispered words of encouragement. One of them said: "Courage, if the Lord gives a burden, he also gives the strength to carry it." And the other said: "Don't be afraid, the whole world is praying for the new pope." Then, when the moment came, I accepted it.' On the third or the fourth ballot (if one took place) Luciani appears to have obtained a clear majority. Cardinal Suenens indicated in interviews with Belgian papers that by the fourth ballot there was 'an extraordinary, unexpected majority, a royal three-quarters'. A three-quarters vote of the 111 cardinals taking part would amount to 84, so it looks as though probably as many as 90 cardinals voted for Luciani on the final ballot. No really strong contender emerged against him—the only cardinal who did well at all was Cardinal Siri, who is thought to have obtained 25 votes on the first ballot and then disappeared from the scene. This lack of challenge and the swift approach to near unanimity undoubtedly increased the feeling within the confines of the conclave that the Holy Spirit was at work.

Cardinal Höffner of Cologne went so far as to suggest that there was unanimity in the final ballot. In a pastoral letter to his diocese he declared: 'There was no need to count the names because the only name read out by the scrutineers was that of Luciani.' More mundane explanations for Luciani's strength than the intervention of the Holy Spirit may respectfully be put forward, for example the strong support coming from the Curia, the patronage of Cardinal Benelli, the backing of the Latin American cardinals who knew of Luciani's concern with the Third World, and the support of the liberal prelates of the north. However this may be, Cardinal Hume summed up the feelings of the cardinals when he said on emerging the following day: 'Seldom have I had such an experience of the presence of God. . . . I am not one for whom the dictates of the Holy Spirit are self-evident . . . but for me he was God's candidate.' The new pope had a rather different comment when he took his place of honour in the Sistine Chapel: 'God will forgive you for what you have done to me.'

POPE JOHN PAUL I

The new pope at once captivated the Romans and initiated his pontificate by displaying a smile big enough to satisfy even Father Greeley. To this he added an informality that endeared him to the people after the northern starchiness and shyness of his predecessor. He had another asset—a skull cap which was always delightfully in disarray with a little quiff of hair showing. As Cardinal Hume commented gaily: 'It suggests a degree of incompetence that is not threatening.' At a mass celebrated at 9.30 on the morning of Sunday 27 August with the Sacred College present, the Pope sketched out the programme for his reign—his desire for continuity, his willingness to implement the decisions of the Council, his support for collegiality, his determination to carry through the revision of canon law to a successful conclusion, his intention to intensify the missionary work of the Church and to continue the ecumenical dialogue, and to promote peace amongst all men of goodwill.

The Pope's determination to avoid any revival of triumphalism was further indicated by his inaugural mass, which I was privileged to attend, and which took place in St Peter's Square on the evening of 3 September. The Pope was determined that there should be no coronation and no enthronement: the papal tiara which had been associated with popes from medieval times and had been used to crown Paul VI was abandoned. Instead the stress was laid upon his position as Bishop of Rome and therefore supreme pastor of the Church: the mass was simply one of the inauguration of this ministry. Thus occurred what was destined to be the most important act of Pope John Paul I's brief pontificate. Instead of stressing his kingly power or such unscriptural titles as 'Vicar of Christ', the Pope was presenting himself as the leader of his fellow bishops. The gesture was symbolic but none the less important for that. As I glanced over at the gold and red plush pen which contained the representatives of the other Churches including many non-Roman Catholic bishops, I realized how much easier it would be without the tiara to leap over that little wall and establish a true communion.

The Pope concelebrated the mass with his cardinals, greeting each of them personally at the end of the ceremony in a visible demonstration of collegiality in the Church. Of course there were moments of high pageantry too: the two Catholic Queens present from Spain and Belgium, as well as the Grand Duchess of Luxemburg, exercised their prerogative of wearing white. The Duke of Norfolk appeared splendid in scarlet. The Swiss Guard were also in multi-coloured splendour although the Noble Guard had vanished in the previous reign. As the purples and blues of the warm summer night gathered in the sky, casting the piazza into shadow, the television lights lit up the altar itself and the surrounding congregation. It was a beautiful and moving scene.

Pope John Paul I continued to endear himself to the pilgrims and others who thronged St Peter's and the Vatican. He won their hearts by his homely addresses. An edition of his letters to such unlikely figures as Charles Dickens, G. K. Chesterton and Pinocchio was published. From time to time came startling theological references inserted in his speeches, including one to 'God, the Mother'. Outwardly the Pope remained smiling and sunny, but there were signs of strain. In fact he felt isolated and alone, his voice at times cracked or rose to a high pitch, the 'impromptus' became more difficult to produce. He confided to Cardinal Villot that he felt ill and tired, and received the kindly advice that he should take regular exercise in the Vatican gardens and not sit for long hours at his desk, otherwise his legs and feet would swell up. There were some tears as well. Of all this the enthusiastic public knew nothing; they were still entranced by the novelty of such a very human personality. His homily was sincere and profound, qualities illustrated by words he wrote before being elevated to the papal chair: 'I must explain that, just as there are different writers, so there are different bishops. Some resemble eagles, who soar with high level magisterial documents. Others are like nightingales who sing the praises of the Lord in a marvellous fashion. Others, instead, are poor wrens, who, on the lowest branch of the episcopal tree, only squeak. I am one of the latter kind.'

On 5 September came a sinister and dramatic omen when the Metropolitan Nikodim of Leningrad, one of the leading ecumenists of the Russian Orthodox Church, collapsed and died in the Pope's presence. Was it a warning?

Pope John Paul I

THE DEATH OF JOHN PAUL I

On the morning of 29 September 1978, I got off the sleeper at Paddington after a day spent in delivering speeches on education in the West Country—I held the Shadow Cabinet portfolio at the time. I came back to my house in Montpelier Square to be greeted in an agitated manner by my housekeeper crying, 'The Pope is dead.' Thinking she was referring to Paul VI, I said, 'Well, of course, we know all about that.' 'No, no,' she said, 'it is the present Pope who is dead, Pope John Paul.' A few days later I found myself at London airport, once again on my way to Rome, and in the company of Cardinal Hume together with the Church of Ireland Archbishop of Dublin, and the Anglican Bishop of London, Dr Gerald Ellison.

The funeral took place that afternoon Wednesday 4 October. Pope John Paul I had been lying in state until late that morning in dignity and splendour, but with the sad sight of the red slippers on his feet, their turned-up soles scarcely worn.

In spite of the rain the authorities decided to hold the funeral outside the basilica in St Peter's Square. There was no time to arrange any new protocol, so the ceremony followed exactly that laid down by Paul VI for his own obsequies. Pope John Paul I's coffin lay on the steps where a few weeks earlier he had been installed; an open volume of the New Testament had been placed upon it and an Easter candle flickered fitfully by its side. The congregation was equally uncomfortable standing in the pouring rain, unable to sit down because of the puddles that had collected on their seats. At the high altar the requiem was led by the eighty-five-year-old Cardinal Confalonieri, the canopy held above his head containing a great and precarious pool of water. In his panegyric he compared the dead pope to 'a meteor that unexpectedly lights up the heavens and disappears'. The coffin was then hoisted on to broad shoulders and carried towards the basilica. As it reached the door it paused for a moment before disappearing, and the rain-sodden crowd gave the one-month pope a farewell round of applause. I realized that within that month I had witnessed all three stages of a papal reign: the election, the inauguration and the burial. Next day I went down to the grotto underneath St Peter's to pay my tribute. To my amazement I found the tomb already complete, flanked by ancient grey marble angels and the name John Paul I engraved on its front. *Sint lacrimae rerum et mentem mortalium tangunt.*

THE ELECTION OF JOHN PAUL II

What was now to be done? An unprecedented crisis faced the Church, but the motto, 'The King is dead, long live the King', applies as much to ecclesiastical as to secular monarchies and the new conclave went ahead, opening on the first possible day under the Pauline rules, Saturday 14 October. Once again the solemn ceremonies were gone through. The mass was celebrated invoking the guidance of the Holy Spirit, outsiders were expelled from the electoral area, and the cardinal electors were sealed off from the external world. The trappings and ritual may have been the same as at the earlier conclave, but the mood was a very different one. The cardinals knew that they had to produce a convincing answer to the problem confronting them. They had loaded the whole burden of the Church's future, with its attendant problems, on to Cardinal Luciani and he had collapsed under the weight. Cynics could hardly suppress their smiles at all the talk there had been about the intervention of the Holy Spirit. These doubts were shared by the not so cynical as well. The events had greatly disturbed me personally and I went off to discuss the whole issue with my friend Cardinal Suenens. I suggested tentatively that one might regard Cardinal Luciani's election to the papacy as a personal mark of favour from God and that having done his work of restoring the papacy's human face he was then called home. The world had seen that a pope could smile and be filled with hope and a kindly providence had ended the reign before the smile faded. Cardinal Suenens listened patiently to my outpourings and then commented: 'You will not see the significance of this pope until you learn the name of his successor—then it will be plain.' Prophetic words!

Before the cardinals entered the conclave for the second time they were speaking much more freely than the first time around. In August only the Curia and conservative prelates had really organized themselves, but on the second occasion other groups followed their example. The other major change from August was the influence being exercised both positively and negatively by the late pope. His was the unseen presence at the conclave. The door left open when he departed could not be closed. 'The world has shown that it wants a pastoral pope, and we must give it another one,' said one cardinal on arriving at Rome airport. But a spiritual shepherd was no longer regarded as enough. The cardinals were aware that they needed someone not only with charismatic appeal but able to cope with the complicated task of governing the Church and dealing with the Curia. There was also a consensus emerging that a pope was wanted who, while accepting the teaching of the Second Vatican Council, would provide a steadying hand at the helm. Above all the cardinals were aware of the necessity of electing a man in full vigour and in good health: another *débâcle* was unthinkable.

THE SECOND CONCLAVE

Once again 111 cardinals were taking part in the conclave—Cardinal Wright, who had been ill during the earlier conclave, took the place of Cardinal Luciani. The favourites of earlier times, whose names had been so sedulously canvassed in the press, were no longer in the headlines. They were, in that hard but expressive Italian word '*bruciati*', burnt-out cases.

This sifting out of the Italian claimants made the emergence of a non-Italian pope a real possibility, and even before the conclave opened, Cardinal Hume's name was seriously canvassed with the support of a leading article in *The Times*. Cardinal Wojtyla's was not but he seems to have received a handful of votes in the first conclave. Certainly when he received in Warsaw the news of John Paul I's death he became uncharacteristically moody and tense and may well have had a premonition of what was to come. Amongst the Italians, Cardinal Benelli was now a serious candidate. His undoubted vigour and energy were an asset, but the memories of those who had suffered at his hands when he was in the Secretariat of State remained an obstacle. Cardinal Siri of Genoa was also a powerful candidate, in spite of his extremely conservative views. While it was known that he had done reasonably well in the first election, his chances were set back severely by the publication of a personal interview in the *Gazzetta del Popolo*. This interview had been given on condition that it should only appear after the electors were safely sealed up in the conclave, but unfortunately for Cardinal Siri it was published on the Saturday, so that the cardinals were able to read it before they became incommunicado. In it he showed himself as ambitious and bad tempered, dismissing John Paul I as an insignificant creature dominated by Vatican officials. The incident severely damaged his chances.

It seems that on the first day of the conclave a sharp struggle took place between the supporters of Cardinal Siri and Cardinal Benelli, reflecting a clash between the conservatives and the progressives. Possibly on the third ballot Cardinal Benelli reached his peak, and he may well have come within 20 votes of the necessary two-thirds plus one majority. After that his support fell away, and as the Italians were unable to put up a united front, their vote splintered. Cardinal Wojtyla was a candidate from the start and enjoyed powerful support, including that of Cardinal König, Archbishop of Vienna. On the second day Wojtyla's support increased in the early ballots and there seems little doubt that he gained the support not only of individuals like Cardinal Hume, but also of the Third World cardinals. The North American cardinals provided a further solid group of supporters. On the seventh ballot Cardinal Wojtyla is said to have really taken off and he secured a decisive majority of 90 votes on the eighth and final ballot of the conclave.

Meanwhile, back in the Piazza, the people waited as the twilight rapidly faded into the darkness of the southern night and a great orange moon rose over the colonnades of St Peter's. On this occasion the smoke signals really did work. The black was black and the white was white, and at nineteen minutes past six on the evening of Monday 16 October it was undoubtedly white smoke that came belching out of the Sistine chimney. Just under half an hour later, at 6.44, Cardinal Felici appeared upon the St Peter's balcony again and declared once more: '*Annuncio vobis gaudium magnum: habemus papam, eminentissimum ac reverendissimum Dominum Carolum, Sanctae Romanae ecclesiae cardinalum Wojtyla, qui sibi nomen imposuit Ioannem Paulum Secundum.*' At first there was a silence as the crowd took the message in, then came an outbreak of tremendous enthusiasm—the Church had a Polish pope for the first time in its history; and for the first time for 450 years a non-Italian would reign in the Vatican. At fifty-eight, Wojtyla was the youngest pope to be elected since Pio Nono came to the papal throne in 1846 at the age of fifty-four. Pio Nono, it should be remembered, reigned for 31 years and 7 months, the longest papal reign since that of St Peter.

At 7.22 the new pope himself appeared and aroused enthusiastic, indeed rapturous applause. He addressed the crowd in the first person and in excellent Italian: 'Praise be Jesus Christ! Dear brothers and sisters we are all still saddened at the death of our beloved Pope John Paul I, so the cardinals have called for a new Bishop of Rome. They called him from a far distant country—far and yet always close because of our communion in faith and Christian tradition. I was afraid to accept that responsibility, yet I do so in a spirit of obedience to the Lord and total faithfulness to Mary, our most holy mother.' Then came both a human and a humourous touch: 'I am speaking to you in your—no, *our* Italian language. If I make mistakes you will have to correct me.' This aroused ecstatic applause.

The Pope concluded: 'I would like to invite you to join me in professing our faith, our hope and our fidelity to Mary, the Mother of Christ and of the Church, and also to begin again on the road of history and of the Church. I begin with the help of God and the help of man.' The new Pope's choice of name, though not unexpected, was significant. The dynasty of the Piuses which had dominated the Church since the time of Pio Nono in 1846 down to the death of Pius XII in 1958 had gone. The new dynasty of John XXIII, Paul VI and their brief hyphenated successor had taken on a fresh lease of life.

POPE JOHN PAUL II OUTLINES HIS PONTIFICATE

On 17 October, speaking in Latin to the cardinals, during a mass in the Sistine Chapel, the Pope made the first major pronouncement of his pontificate. He made it clear that his policy would be one of continuity and stressed the importance of adhering to the Second Vatican Council: 'We consider, therefore, our primary duty that of promoting, with prudent but encouraging action, the most exact execution of the norms and the directives of the Council. Above all we favour the development of a proper mentality.' He singled out collegiality, the joint government of the Church by the Pope and the bishops, as being of supreme importance: 'Collegiality undoubtedly means that there will be appropriate development of those bodies, sometimes new, sometimes updated, which can secure a better union of heart, of will, of activity in building up the body of Christ which is the Church. In this regard we make special mention of the synod of bishops, first established before the Council came to an end by that man of immense genius Paul VI.' While stressing the primacy of love, the Pope also declared that faithfulness indicated respect for what he called 'the great discipline of the Church', before going on to pledge himself to the ecumenical cause: 'We intend, therefore, to proceed along the way already begun, by favouring those steps which serve to remove obstacles. Hopefully, then, thanks to a common effort we might arrive finally at full communion.'

Pope John Paul II

The Pope declared his intention of working with all men of good will for a permanent peace and the development of international justice. At the same time he expressly excluded any intention of political interference or of 'participation in the working out of temporal affairs'.

That same afternoon, the Pope gave an early sign of his independence when he left the Vatican to visit the Gemelli Hospital, where his friend Bishop Deskur was seriously ill. On 29 October the Pope took off by helicopter to pay homage to the twelfth-century statue of Our Lady at Mentrolle, thirty miles from Rome—the sanctuary is looked after by Polish nuns.

A further sign that the Pope knew his own mind came over his insistence that the letter M for Mary should be included in his coat of arms. The prelate who designed the Pope's arms, Archbishop Bruno Heim, the apostolic delegate in Great Britain, and the leading authority on ecclesiastical heraldry, stated that the use of letters was out of accord with 'heraldic tradition and diction' and described it as reminding him of a 'commercial advertisement or trademark'. He expressed his views strongly to the Pope but the latter was determined to pay honour to Mary whatever the niceties of heraldic protocol, and his will prevailed. In his arms, prominent in the right-hand corner, stands a large capital M, placed at the foot of the cross in the shield, to commemorate Mary's own presence in a similar position at the crucifixion.

The Pope's inaugural mass took place on the morning of Sunday 22 October, and followed the pattern of Pope John Paul I's induction, with one significant difference. The Archbishop of Canterbury, Dr Donald Coggan, attended the mass, the first Archbishop of Canterbury to be present at such a function since the Reformation. During his address the Pope spoke movingly of his love for his country: 'To you, my dear fellow countrymen, what shall I say? Everything that I could say fades into insignificance compared to what my heart feels and your hearts feel at this moment. So let us leave aside words. Let there remain just a great silence before God, the silence that turns into prayer. I ask you: be with me on the white mountain and in every other place.' (His allusion to the white mountain is a reference to Jasna Góra, on which stands the monastery of Czestochowa with its icon of the Virgin Mary.)

The Pope showed his real mastery of languages when he spoke not only in the traditional languages of French, German, English and Spanish, but also in Czech, Ukrainian, Lithuanian and Russian. The cardinals came up to pay their homage and each one was given a great bear hug of an embrace and a little homily. The papal ceremony lasted for nearly four hours until it was at last brought to an end by the Pope with the homely words: 'It is time for lunch for you and also for the Pope.'

The Calling of the Man from a Far Country

THE PATH TO ROME

The man who made history on that warm October night in the Piazza San Pietro was born in the little country town of Wadowice on Tuesday 18 May 1920. (By coincidence I share the same birth day with the Pope, although not the same year. In the old rhyme we are told that Tuesday's child is 'full of grace'.) Wadowice has some industry including a paperworks and a factory which supplies spare parts for motors, but it remains primarily a market town and a centre for the peasant population of the surrounding countryside. In the baptismal register of the parish church there is an entry which at first sight looks similar to many others: 'Karolus Josef, born to Karol Wojtyla and his wife Emilia (born Kaczorowska) on May 18 1920' with the date of the baptism given as 20 June of the same year. At that point the entry starts to look somewhat different. There is the following succinct and unique litany:

1.11.46, Priest
28.9.58, Bishop
30.12.63, Archbishop of Cracow
26.6.67, Cardinal
16.10.78, in Summum Pontificem electus, Joannes Paulus II.

The new baby was born into a military family. His father, also called Karol, was a junior officer in the Polish Army and worked as an administrative military official in Wadowice. Karol had an elder brother who studied as a doctor but who died before the war. On 13 April 1929, when Karol was only nine, tragedy struck the family when his mother Emilia died at the early age of forty-five. Perhaps it was from this traumatic experience that the future pope's devotion to Mary grew.

The family inhabited a modest three-room apartment without a bath, which can still be seen. Karol or Karolek or Lolek, as he soon came to be known, led the normal life of a Polish boy of his age and background. He attended the local high school where his academic record was good. Already he was keen on sport and was an enthusiastic footballer, making an excellent goalkeeper, we are told by contemporaries. He liked all forms of sport; walking, canoeing, swimming and, above all, skiing. The young Lolek was most at home in the mountains: he might have said with Wordsworth: 'In the mountains do we feel our faith.' At school, too, his early capacity for and interest in acting appeared, and he showed a youthful talent for dancing. In 1938 the family moved to Cracow itself, then, as now, a uniquely beautiful medieval city, and he began the study of Polish literature at the Jagiellonian University, founded many centuries before in 1364 by Kasimir the Great. Here he studied not only the Polish language and literature but philosophy as well, and it was at the university that his acting

Papal coat of arms displayed in Mexico, 1979

talent really began to flourish. Wojtyla joined a student acting group and in his free time studied for a diploma in drama. As contemporary photographs show, he was a strikingly handsome youth and his fellow students testify to the quality of his beautiful speaking voice.

In 1939 Karol's student days were interrupted by the outbreak of the war. Poland was partitioned between the forces of Germany moving in from the west and the Russians from the east. The young Wojtyla, however, was despite the chaos able to continue his acting. He joined the Rhapsodic Theatre Group (Teatr Rapsodyczny) founded by Mieczyslaw Kotlarczyk, which presented Polish classics and developed its own particular style of poetic declamation. The theatre became a means of resistance to the invaders and these experiences account for the Pope's later insistence on the importance of culture in preserving the life of a nation.

Students were in danger of deportation to work camps by the Nazis, as indeed were intellectuals; thus the entire faculty of the university was dispatched to concentration camps in June 1940. Karol escaped by going into hiding. In 1941 his father died, a further profound bereavement and Karol took up work in a stone quarry and then in a chemical plant. His experiences in the stone quarry produced a poem, *The Quarry*, published in 1957:

> *Hands are the heart's landscape. They split sometimes*
> *Like ravines into which an undefined force rolls.*
> *The very same hands which man only opens*
> *When his palms have had their fill of toil.*
> *Now he sees: because of him alone, others can walk in peace.*

Mary Craig, in her biography *Man from a Far Country* (Hodder and Stoughton, 1979), writes: '*The Stone Quarry* contains all the themes which would come to characterise his ministry: the immense compassion, the sensitivity to human dignity, the respect for manual labour, the longing to serve, the awareness of love as the driving force of life, and the perception of a Reality that transcends the observable world.'

The anonymity of the stone quarry and the factory provided young Wojtyla with a protection but the acting still went on. Plays were performed in a private apartment and remained an important part of the cultural resistance.

During his period at the Solvey chemical works, Wojtyla suffered two serious accidents. On the first occasion he was knocked down by a tram and fractured his skull. Illness and convalescence gave time for reflection and it was during this period that he experienced his first call to the priesthood. A few months later he had a second brush with death when he was involved in an accident with a truck. Again the call to the priesthood sounded, and he determined to respond to it as soon as was feasible. In 1942 he joined the Theological

Department at the Jagiellonian University, an illegal and proscribed organization. Two years later he suddenly disappeared from the Solvey chemical factory, and did not surface in public again until after the war. This disappearance has led to some highly romantic speculations that during this period the future pope was married and then widowed. The truth—alas—is rather more prosaic: Wojtyla was taken into the palace of Cardinal Sapieha, the Archbishop of Cracow, to save him from the Gestapo and enable him to continue his theological studies. In January 1945, the future pope was able to come out of hiding and on 1 November 1946, at the age of twenty-six, he was ordained a priest.

After ordination, Wojtyla was sent to Rome to study for two years at the Angelicum University, taking up residence at the Belgian College. Father Wojtyla took as the subject of his thesis 'The Concept of Faith in the Writings of St John of the Cross'. His director of studies was the redoubtable Père Reginald Garrigou-Lagrange, a Dominican, a Thomist and a confirmed traditionalist. From what must have been a restrictive atmosphere the young priest escaped in the summer of 1947 for an extended visit to France where he linked up with the worker-priest movement and the young Christian workers.

In 1948 he returned to Cracow to take up a position as curate and immersed himself in parish work, but in 1951 he was granted a two-year sabbatical to continue his studies at the Catholic University of Lublin. Father Wojtyla had long been interested not only in mysticism but in moral theology and the subject of his thesis on this occasion was 'The Possibility of Building a System of Catholic Ethics on the Basis of Max Scheler'.

Scheler (1874–1928) was a personalist philosopher, whose approach to reality was phenomenological, concentrating on the experience and consciousness of the self. Love, Scheler held, of which God is the origin, constitutes the great principle of human relationships. Scheler maintained that the person cannot be defined on the basis of existence alone because that does not distinguish human beings sufficiently from things—the person in his view was constituted by values. Man is thus in a state of continual development and activity, so that what is important is not what persons 'are', but what they 'become', as they realize values concretely in their lives. One can see how such an approach would appeal to Wojtyla but it was not immediately reconcilable with Thomist concepts, and this thesis set out to bring this about. The influence of Scheler can be seen in his later writings, particularly in *Love and Responsibility* published in 1960. Wojtyla's theme in that book is the essentially unselfish nature of true love between a man and a woman, a love which is self giving and not mutually exploiting.

Again, it is human relationships which form the substance of his play *In Front of the Jeweller's Shop*, which was published in the same year under his pen name of Andrzej Jawien and was broadcast in 1980 by the BBC. Wojtyla was also publishing poetry in these years, his first poem, *Song of the Brightness of Water*, appearing in 1950. In 1954 he was appointed Professor of Moral Philosophy at the University of Lublin and was also teaching in a Cracow seminary, as well as acting as chaplain to the students. During these years a continual struggle raged between the Church and the Communist regime in which Wojtyla was involved, but it was not until 1958 when he was appointed auxiliary Bishop of Cracow that he moved into the front line.

At this moment there was a lull in the struggle and Wojtyla, finding himself at thirty-eight the youngest bishop in the country, was given time to find his feet. In 1962 he was present as bishop at the first session of the Vatican Council, making two interventions, one on liturgy and the other on the sources of revelation. In the following session, on 23 September 1963, he made an important intervention in the debate on the nature of the Church, insisting that the Church should be envisaged as 'the people of God before there was any discussion of the ecclesiastical hierarchy'. Another notable contribution was his forthright support for the declaration on religious liberty. What these speeches show is not that Bishop Wojtyla was an advanced progressive but that he was a man reasonably open-minded on the theological issues of the day. He became a member of the mixed commission dealing with the document 'The Church in the Modern World', and when disputes broke out over the description of the document, the compromise of calling it 'A Pastoral Constitution' came from Bishop Wojtyla.

In 1963, at the age of forty-three, he was appointed Archbishop of Cracow and indeed had been acting Archbishop some time before this. He was much concerned during this period with family problems and set up a family institute to study them. He was forthright in his condemnation of abortion which had been legalized in Poland in 1957 and he was equally strongly opposed to contraception. Although rigid on moral–theological matters, Archbishop Wojtyla was much more flexible in the political sphere, and this willingness to compromise was frequently contrasted with the more rigid stance of the Cardinal Primate, Cardinal Wyszynski. Archbishop Wojtyla was aware of the danger of a wedge being driven between himself and the Primate which would immediately be exploited by the Communist Government and so while putting his own point of view in private he was always punctilious in maintaining a display of complete unity in public.

On 26 June 1967, Archbishop Wojtyla was created a cardinal by Paul VI. He busied himself with applying the lessons of the Council to his diocese in Poland. On social issues he remained outspoken, defending the Jews strongly in 1968 against Communist attacks. He maintained contact with all in his diocese by having an open day when people could call without an appointment and were

received on a first come, first served basis. His links with students remained strong and he began to organize for a pastoral synod for his diocese of Cracow to start its deliberations in 1971 and continue indefinitely.

Cardinal Wojtyla was well known in Rome through his service on a number of commissions, and had, through his book *Love and Responsibility*, been asked to serve on the special group of prelates and theologians who had been considering the traditional Catholic teaching on birth control. The sixteen cardinals and bishops on the commission held a special meeting in June 1966 to vote on the draft report which approved a change but Archbishop Wojtyla was not present, an absence which has never been satisfactorily explained. He was also a regular attender at the synods which were held during these years and in 1971 was elected to the synod's permanent council. He had been on the Council of the Laity since 1967 and in 1974, at the synod, put forward a position paper on the theological implications of evangelization. In 1976 he was asked to give the Lenten retreat for the Pope and his household, a singular mark of distinction. These conferences were published in the same year under the title *Segno Di Contradizione*.

Cardinal Wojtyla may have come from a country far away from Rome, but by the time he came to be elected to the papacy he was well known in the ecclesiastical circles of the eternal city. He was also known to a wider circle through his travels. In 1970 he visited Australia for the Eucharistic Congress and in 1976 he was present at another Eucharistic Congress in Philadelphia. He paid another visit to the United States and has also been to Canada. All these travels had a spiritual purpose: the way was being prepared for the world-wide mission of his papal years.

5

The Pope and the Church

————— ✠ —————

The Pope, like Janus, has two faces: one is turned to the Church of which he is
the governor and head, the other to the world, to mankind in general, the beings
who carry together the burden of their shared humanity. It is not too fanciful to
see this double function symbolized in the traditional blessing which all Popes
give on solemn occasions: '*Urbi et Orbi*', to the city and to the world. Rome, of
course, is the secular city referred to, but it is also an image of the ecclesiastical
city of the Church. To understand the role of the pope in the modern world one
has to see him under both these aspects. The Pope's face turned towards the
world has already been displayed in the account of John Paul's journeys; it is
time now to look more closely at his attitude to his Church.

One criticism of the Pope emerging with increasing insistence is that whereas
he is indefatigable in asserting the rights of the Church and defending them
against the totalitarian State, his attitude to members of his own flock is of a
different order. They are expected to accept and to conform to his declarations of
authority, and in the last resort their only course is to obey or suffer ecclesiastical
penalties. There is certainly something in this accusation of double standards,
but the different papal attitudes become more comprehensible if they are seen as
reflections of the double aspects of the Pope's own formation.

Pope John Paul's social outlook is progressive—he is the only pope who has
grown up entirely outside the capitalist system and in a society experiencing
continual conflict between the rights of the State and the Church. His champion-
ship of the freedoms and rights of the Polish Church has obliged him to assert
not only Catholic rights against the State but human rights in general. The Polish
Church has been made a highly conservative Church, in part because of this
struggle. It has clung to Rome as a safeguard and sees the walls of the Vatican
not as a prison, but as a bastion for its defence. The Pope's own theological
training has been of a traditional character both in Poland and in Rome. Indeed

his religious culture appears in some ways to be as narrow as his secular culture is broad. Catholic intellectuals in particular have been critical of a number of the Pope's attitudes. How far are these accusations and reservations justified? Perhaps the best way of essaying an answer is to take a closer look at some of the issues in contemporary Catholicism and the Pope's handling of them.

ECUMENISM

Ecumenism—the movement for reconciliation between the Christian Churches —which, starting in Protestantism at the beginning of the century, has spread to the heart of the Roman Catholic Communion, provides a good starting point. The ecumenical movement is probably the most hopeful development for centuries in the Christian body. Rome stood aloof from all such efforts until the coming of Pope John. The official attitude until Pope John and his Council was that unity already existed in the Roman Catholic Church and that all that was needed for others to achieve it was submission to her decisions. Pope John leapt over these theological barriers by opening his heart and mind to other Christians. The setting up of the Secretariat for Christian Unity in Rome institutionalized his generous impulses. The Secretariat, headed first by Cardinal Bea and then by Cardinal Willerbrands, has since then been the focus of all Catholic ecumenical effort. The movement, which was given such an impetus by Pope John, was consolidated under Pope Paul but has now to some extent moved into the doldrums. It will be a crucial test of the present pontificate whether ecumenism will be able to resume its onward march.

There can be no doubt about Pope Paul's sincere support for ecumenism as such. It was a subject he turned to in the very first address of his reign, that to the cardinals on 17 October 1978: 'Nor at this point must we forget the brethren of other Churches and Christian Confessions. For the cause of ecumenism is so lofty and such a sensitive issue that we may not keep silent about it. How often do we meditate together on the last wish of Christ, who asked the Father for the gift of unity for the disciples? Who does not remember how much St Paul stressed "the unity of the Spirit", from which the followers of Christ might have the same love, being "of one accord, of one mind"? Therefore one can hardly credit that a deplorable division still exists among Christians. This is a cause of embarrassment and perhaps a scandal to others. And so we wish to proceed along the road which has happily been opened and to encourage whatever can serve to remove the obstacles, desirous as we are, that through common effort full communion may eventually be achieved.'

What this declaration will amount to in practice is not yet clear, but certain signs are emerging. First, the Pope clearly feels it an essential part of his mission

Hosts ready for the moment of consecration at a papal mass

to reassert in unequivocal terms the identity of the Roman Catholic Church. In his address to the American bishops in the United States, he declared that the Church's unity 'subsists indestructibly in the Catholic Church' The use of the word 'subsists', a conciliar term, was significant in that the Pope was explicitly adopting a term less exclusive than 'exists'. But he went on to reject inter-communion as the answer to the Church's prayer for perfect unity. Here he was supporting the view that communion is a sign of unity not a means towards bringing it about. The same point was made by Cardinal Hume when addressing the General Synod of the Church of England at Church House on 1 February 1978. He said: 'We believe that this sharing presupposes not only the same belief in the reality of Christ's presence in the sacred species, but also a common faith in general. I do not question for one moment that the desire for so many to share the same eucharist is anything but a gift from God, a gift which impels us now to work all the harder for the resolution of our difficulties. This desire is present in every Christian Church and community throughout the land. But as our official response to the ten propositions of the Churches' Unity Commission shows, we recognize that there are other questions to be resolved before we can, as Churches, approach the altar of the Lord together.'

Those who take a contrary view to the Pope's and Cardinal Hume's stress that what is important is baptism. They argue that once it has been conceded that baptism admits to the mystical body of Christ then it follows logically that the members should also be admitted to Holy Communion. There are not two bodies, one baptismal and one eucharistic, but only one, the mystical body of Christ. Once that has been established, the argument for shared communion logically follows. The English Catholic bishops' response to the ten propositions of the Churches' Unity Commission, which itself suggests a covenant committing to inter-communion, states that 'Baptized members of other Churches are truly incorporated into the crucified and glorified Christ', and goes on to say that: 'Baptism manifests the visible unity of the one Church of Christ which the risen Lord himself constitutes and gives.' The response goes on to state that the other Churches are 'in partial but real communion with the Roman Catholic Church'. This statement raises more questions than it answers. What, for example, does the concept of 'partial but real communion' mean? Furthermore, it is difficult to see how baptized persons are members of the body of Christ in one sense and not in another. These complexities remain to be resolved.

It was in Washington, too, that the Pope stressed that agreement not only on faith but on morals is essential for unity. In a reference to Protestantism he declared: 'In this context, recognition must be given to the deep division which still exists over moral and ethical matters. The moral life and the life of faith are so deeply united that it is impossible to divide them.' This sort of remark is typical of the Pope's cautious approach to ecumenism. Warnings and reservations are expressed when addressing the Churches of the West but they are notably absent when addressing the Orthodox Churches of the East. These Churches, furthermore, would have much less difficulty in coming to terms with the Pope's Mariology than the Reformation Churches.

In speaking of ecumenism the Pope often stresses that it is as much a spiritual as a theological movement. Such an attitude is by no means negative to ecumenical advance: indeed it may facilitate it. An ecumenism centred on ecclesiology can have only a limited appeal and if exaggerated may well approximate to a new form of idolatry. A Christocentric ecumenical movement on the other hand avoids this danger and commands a wide appeal amongst the laity and those who do not live habitually in a theological world. The Pope accordingly may well be wise in stressing that the way forward is more about 'spiritual renewal' than theological compromise. In this too he is being faithful to the Second Vatican Council, which declared: 'There can be no ecumenism worthy of the name without interior conversion. For it is from newness of attitudes of mind, from self denial and unstinted love, that desires of unity take their rise and develop in a mature way' (see *Decree on Ecumenism*). The charismatic renewal movement with its stress on a fundamental conversion to Jesus Christ has an increasingly important role to play in the ecumenical movement.

A basic question which still needs to be clarified is the theological basis on which the Pope perceives unity coming about. If it means a simple submission to Rome, then the prospects for ecumenism are somewhat bleak. On the other hand, if the Pope's approach is sufficiently flexible to allow for the historical dimension of division, and the need to have a similar period for full healing and reconciliation, the story could unfold in quite another way. Certainly there were encouraging signs of papal flexibility and sensitivity in the address made during his visit to the Patriarch Dimitrios at Istanbul. The Pope was careful to express himself in Orthodox rather than in Latin juridical terms. Peter, for example, was described as the 'chorus leader of the apostles', a phrase which his hearers would have been familiar with from their own liturgy. He was further presented not as the embryonic Vicar of Christ, but as 'a brother among brothers . . . entrusted with the task of confirming them in their faith'. The Pope's mission was to ensure 'the harmony of apostolic preaching'. Presented in this way as a primacy of service rather than one of jurisdiction, the Holy See becomes not an obstacle to unity but an essential ingredient of its creation.

ORTHODOXY

The Pope's first priority in the ecumenical field is reconciliation with the Orthodox Churches. For Rome, Orthodoxy presents itself as 'the problem of problems'. It is arguable that it was the schism of 1054 which led directly to the Reformation, and thus to the split in the western Church. Had the rift with Orthodoxy not occurred, Rome would not have been able to embark on the course of imposing a juridical uniformity which led directly to the northern European revolt. Orthodoxy is, furthermore, a religion of which the Pope has had direct experience in Poland—Protestantism by contrast is somewhat remote—and with his somewhat Gaullist view of a Europe not confined to the west but stretching to the Urals, Orthodoxy is bound to loom large. Orthodoxy does not present the theological difficulties inherent in any *rapprochement* with western Protestantism and with which the Pope's background does not fit him especially well to deal. On matters of the validity of orders, the essentials of the mass, devotion to the Virgin, there is a wide measure of agreement between the two Communions. Married clergy present a difficulty but this is quite capable of accommodation despite the Pope's championing of celibacy. As to women priests, Orthodox opposition is even fiercer than that of Rome. Some difficulties could arise about divorce, which is recognized under certain conditions in Orthodox Churches, but doubtless the Orthodox would have their own objections to Rome's annulment procedures. Such matters need not hold up intercommunion—there can simply be an agreement to differ.

The real difficulties are partly psychological, the result of centuries of separateness and mistrust, and partly political, fear of the juridical power of Rome. These matters are rather more likely to be resolved by the 'dialogue of love' than by the 'dialogue of truth'. Love casts out not only fear but mistrust as well.

The progress of this dialogue depends to a large extent on the personalities of those involved. Certainly the Pope and the Patriarch have made an encouraging start. There is no denying the warmth of Pope John Paul towards Orthodoxy and the Patriarch Dimitrios has been equally forthcoming. In this respect I recall a visit I paid to the Patriarch Athenagoras in July 1967. We were discussing the role of Paul VI, and the Patriarch commented: 'I call him not Paul VI, but Paul II, for that is what he is, a second Paul, a prophet preparing the way for the unity which is to come.' I raised the question of how the obstacles to unity were to be overcome. The Patriarch replied: 'There are no obstacles to unity.' I was surprised at such a forthright statement and asked about the theological difficulties: 'Surely', I said, 'they exist.' To this the Patriarch replied, 'I often think it strange that all the theologians in every Church seem to have had the same mother.'

Pope John Paul's visit to Istanbul, which has been described earlier, undoubtedly generated warmth and understanding between the two prelates. It bore early fruit when the long-postponed theological dialogue finally opened on the islands of Rhodes and Patmos in June 1980. A year later on Whit Sunday, June

1981, the Pope made a personal appeal for unity between Catholics and Orthodox. The Pope was speaking by means of a tape-recorded message at a service in St Peter's to commemorate the calling of two Councils of the early Church—the First Council of Constantinople in 381 and the Council of Ephesus in 431. The doctrines enunciated by these councils are accepted by both the eastern and western Churches. On this occasion the Pope stressed that it was the Council of Ephesus that defined the role of Mary as the *Theotokos*, the Mother of God. It was notable, too, that he recited the creed as it was formulated at the Council of Constantinople and omitted the subsequent '*filioque*' formulation which led to the split between Constantinople and Rome. The prospects for a reconciliation between Roman Catholicism and Orthodoxy have never looked brighter.

ANGLICANISM

During his encounter with Pope John Paul, the Patriarch Dimitrios stressed that their goal was not a dialogue between two Churches but a union of all Christians. Amongst the Churches the Patriarch had in mind, the Anglican Communion would have figured prominently. Relations between the two Churches have steadily improved in recent years. It is a far cry from the days in the last century when the Patriarch of Constantinople was not quite sure who the Archbishop of Canterbury was! It is fortunate too that Dr Runcie, the present Archbishop of Canterbury, has been active for many years in promoting Orthodox–Anglican unity. At his enthronement in Canterbury Cathedral, the Archbishop made the gesture, later repeated by the Pope, arranging that the '*filioque*' clause, rejected by Orthodoxy, should be omitted from the Creed. It could well be that the Anglican Church will play an important role as a catalyst in facilitating reunion between East and West.

Anglican–Roman Catholic relations have steadily improved since Dr Fisher's historic visit to Rome. Dr Ramsey consolidated the new relationship in his visit of 1966 and the policy of *rapprochement* with Rome was continued by his successor, Dr Donald Coggan. In April 1977 Dr Coggan himself visited Rome, but it was probably the least successful of the three archiepiscopal visits. In the first place it was badly timed: Pope Paul was ageing and unwilling to open up new perspectives. Opposition to the visit within the Vatican was strengthened by a message from the English Roman Catholic hierarchy advising the Pope (quite superfluously) not to be carried away by the Archbishop, and then by a somewhat undiplomatic sermon preached by Dr Coggan in Rome at the Anglican Church of St Paul, in which he called for inter-communion between the two Churches and announced, to the Vatican's astonishment, that in many cases it was already taking place.

The Pope and the Church

Dr Ramsey's visit to Pope Paul in 1966 had led to the setting up of a joint theological commission of members of the Roman Catholic Church and the Anglican Communion. This has published three reports: on the Eucharist, the Ministry and on Authority, reaching a remarkable degree of agreement. 'We believe', declares the first report of 1971 on the Eucharist, 'that we have reached substantial agreement on the doctrine of the eucharist. Although we are all conditioned by the traditional way in which we have expressed and practised our eucharistic faith, we are convinced that if there are any remaining points of disagreement they can be resolved on the principles here established.' The report on the Ministry (1973) displayed equal consensus and set out a joint view on the threefold ministry of bishops, priests and deacons, and on the nature of apostolic succession.

The question of authority in the Church presents the most formidable obstacle to reunion. But even in this minefield the joint report (1976) reveals real progress. Agreement has been reached on the basic principles of authority and primacy although difficulties remain over the meaning and scope of the papal doctrine of infallibility as well as on the papal claim to universal immediate jurisdiction over the whole Church. Doctrinal agreement among theologians cannot of itself achieve the goal of Christian unity but the reports have prepared the way for a notable advance.

A further stage was reached in September 1981 when Dr Runcie, together with the two chairmen of the International Commission—the Archbishop of Dublin, Dr Henry McAdoo, and the Catholic Bishop of East Anglia, the Rt Reverend Alan Clark—announced that the Commission's final report had been agreed. The report dealt with the outstanding issues on Church authority and included consideration of the primacy and infallibility of the pope as well as the papal claim to universal jurisdiction over the Church. The report was to be submitted to Pope John Paul and Dr Runcie and published shortly afterwards.

Thus the Commission has brought to an end twelve years of work, resulting in substantial agreement. All the indications are that a sufficient basis of agreement has been established on the fundamentals of doctrine to provide a basis for reunion between the two Churches. However, the reports still have to be approved by the relevant authorities in each Church, which in the Church of England is the General Synod and in the Catholic Church, the Pope himself.

Whatever the verdict that is eventually passed on the Commission's work, there remain pressing problems that have to be resolved between the two Churches. Foremost amongst these is the question of the validity of Anglican orders and their recognition by the Catholic Church. The Commission may have reached agreement on the concept of ministry at the present day but there remains the stumbling block of the papal bull, *Apostolicae Curiae*, of 1896, which condemned Anglican orders as being null and void. Closely connected with this issue is the question of mutual admission to Holy Communion at the altars of the two Churches. This is not officially countenanced at the moment but it does take place privately and on an increasing number of occasions. Public authority exists for admitting Anglicans to Roman Catholic Communion although not in England. Cardinal Marty, the former Archbishop of Paris, for example, while in office issued a general invitation to Anglicans in France who are unable to attend their own churches to attend and participate in the mass.

The position of Catholics attending and communicating at Anglican services is somewhat more complex. The Anglican discipline as laid down by the General Synod is to admit baptized Christians, including Roman Catholics, to Anglican Holy Communion on an occasional but not a permanent basis. The whole question of inter-communion has to be regulated by the authorities of the two churches, but there is no doubt that individual Catholics and Anglicans are seeking a way forward by the practice of occasional inter-communion amongst themselves.

An issue which has in the past caused considerable difficulties between Anglicans and Roman Catholics has been the Roman Catholic discipline on mixed marriages. This formerly required promises from both the parties that the children would be brought up in the Roman Catholic faith as a condition of allowing a marriage between them. The marriage ceremony could be conducted only by a Catholic priest in a Roman Catholic church. This discipline has been drastically amended. No promises are now required from the non-Catholic partner. The ceremony may take place before a Catholic priest or a Catholic priest acting with an Anglican one and the place of ceremony is to be decided by the parties subject to the approval of the bishop. The only promise required is from the Roman Catholic partner in respect of the upbringing of the children, who has to promise to do all in his or her power—without jeopardizing the marriage—to see that the children are brought up in the Roman Catholic faith. This promise is not wholly acceptable to Anglicans, nor is the ban on the parties communicating at the marriage service. As the Anglican Bishop of Chelmsford, Bishop Trillo, has commented: 'Until the couple are able to receive the sacrament of Holy Communion together, we must doubt the propriety of performing such a wedding in the context of the mass.' (*Marriages between Anglicans and Roman Catholics—a Commentary*, Church Information Office pamphlet)

Further problems likely to cause conflict between the two Churches are a cluster of moral issues such as the attitude to birth control, abortion and divorce, and the question of the ordination of women priests. These, however, need not constitute insuperable obstacles to a reunion since opinion within each of the Churches is divided on the issues, although the official teaching of the Roman Catholic Church is much clearer and more definite than that which prevails in the Anglican Communion, especially on abortion. A final source of difficulty is the ordination of women to the priesthood, but this has still to be resolved within the Church of England and other Churches of the Anglican Communion.

Meanwhile, the usual ecumenical courtesies have continued. In Accra in Ghana on 9 May 1980, the Pope and Dr Runcie had their first meeting. In a joint statement they endorsed the objective of advancing Christian unity: 'Time is too short and the need too pressing to waste Christian energy pursuing old rivalries. . . . the talents and resources of all the Churches must be shared if Christ is to be seen and heard effectively.' The statement derived particular significance by being made in Africa, where division between the Christian Churches is a major obstacle to missionary effort.

In October 1980 the Queen paid a state visit to the Vatican and expressed her approval of 'the growing movement of unity between the Christian Churches', and she went on to refer to the growing dialogue and community of interest

Queen Elizabeth II, with the Duke of Edinburgh, pays a state visit to Pope John Paul II, 1980

between the Anglican and Roman Catholic Churches in the Commonwealth. Pope John Paul's visit to Britain cannot be expected to resolve at a stroke the difficult problems that the two Churches are confronting in their quest for unity, but it will have a symbolic significance and is likely to advance the cause of unity further. The visit will make it easier to resolve some of the difficult issues that Archbishop Runcie raised in a lecture given at Westminster Abbey in 1981. Controversial issues he listed included contraception, the question of a married clergy and the degree of freedom of local Churches from Vatican control. 'Ultimately,' he declared, 'the theological question can be put like this: what is involved and what is not involved in acceptance of the universal ministry of the Bishop of Rome; is this ministry not solely concerned with the basic unity of the faith in the world-wide communion of the Churches and their God-given diversity; would this mean, at the most, a form of universal presidency, in charity where essential matters of faith are at stake; what relation would the Vatican have to the various synods of the Anglican Communion?' (*The Times*, 12 March 1981.)

These questions of Dr Runcie's get to the heart of the matter and they will need to be answered before reunion can be achieved. Perhaps the way forward lies along the recognition of a double role for the Holy See, one in relation to the Roman Catholic Communion itself and another of a different character in relation to the other Christian Churches. Dr Runcie concluded: 'We are now at the stage of dialogue when the hard questions need to be put, and Rome will have some tough questions to put to Anglicans as well. In this exchange both traditions will be purified and renewed.'

DIALOGUES WITH OTHER CHURCHES

The pre-eminence of the Anglican–Roman Catholic dialogue should not lead to an underestimation of the importance of relations between Rome and the other Protestant Churches in Britain. A dialogue is also taking place between Roman Catholics and Methodists, and relations have in recent years grown closer between the Church of Scotland and the Catholic Church. At any rate the asperities and hostilities of the past have been steadily diminishing. The dialogue with the Methodists is being conducted on both an international and a national level, and the representatives of British Catholics and Methodists recently declared, in *Eucharist, Ministry, Authority*: 'The special and on-going responsibility of the Bishop of Rome would be exercised in his calling of, and acting presidency within, a Universal Council of the Church whenever the situation demanded a decision and action by the whole Church. Such a pattern as this might well enable a united Church to fulfil its mission of proclaiming the whole gospel to the whole world.' (Ecumenical Commission, 1981) The dialogue with Methodism illustrates the complexities of the ecumenical movement. English Methodism does not have a clear-cut doctrinal basis nor is it distinguished by theological scholarship, but characteristics of Methodism are the practice of evangelical piety, warmth of religious feeling, strong missionary zeal and social witness. Methodist doctrine is contained more in its hymns than in theological formulations, although it should be noted that the hymns of the Wesleys in particular are based on a high sacramental doctrine.

CHURCH ORDER: MORAL ISSUES

The Pope's conservative stand on moral issues, ranging from birth control through abortion to divorce, became clear to the world through his speeches on his foreign journeys, which supplemented shorter comments made at his weekly Wednesday general audiences in St Peter's. Some observers were surprised at the contrast between the Pope's liberalism in the championing of human rights against totalitarian states, and his conservatism on these other matters, but they need not have been. The Pope had made his attitudes clear in books and lectures long before he came to the papacy. All of his views had been carefully thought through. His unequivocal support, for example, for the encyclical of his predecessor Paul VI, *Humanae Vitae*, was spelt out in an address to a Catholic conference held at Milan in June 1978 to mark the tenth anniversary of the issue of the encyclical. (See *Fruitful and Responsible Love* by Karol Wojtyla, St Paul's Publications, 1978.)

This and his attitudes towards other sexual issues rest on a carefully considered philosophy. Probably no man has come to the papacy with more of his opinions on record than the present Pope. The papal statements on ethics have already been described and need not be recapitulated here, but it may be useful to outline briefly the philosophical basis on which they rest.

This was most fully set out in his book *Love and Responsibility*, based on the lectures he delivered as a professor of moral theology at the Catholic University of Lublin in 1958-9 and published in 1960. The book was revised and republished in 1981 (by Collins). The Holy Father wishes it to be read not as a papal utterance but as one by Karol Wojtyla. *Love and Responsibility* constitutes a major treatise on sexual ethics, dealing with such issues as chastity, birth control, the marriage relationship, the purpose of sexuality, the family and divorce.

Wojtyla's ethical thought is primarily a personalist one. In marriage he sees

Over page: Priests are addressed by the Pope at Notre Dame Cathedral, France 1980

the basis of the relationship as the wellbeing of the parties and the self-revealing of each partner to the other. Marriage, while based on the natural functions of procreation and the care of children, transcends them. Wojtyla contrasts this unselfish self-giving with the utilitarian view of sex and marriage which regards a sexual partner as an object for use. Thus he writes: 'Love in human relationships is not something ready-made. It begins as a principle or idea which people must somehow live up to in their behaviour, which they must desire if they want, as they should, to free themselves from the utilitarian, the "consumer" attitude (Latin *consumere* = use) towards other persons.' This principle in married love required a total and permanent self-giving hence the impossibility of divorce.

Wojtyla defines sinful love as 'simply a relationship between two persons so structured that emotion as such and more particularly pleasure as such have assumed the dimensions of goods in their own right, and are the sole decisive consideration, while no account at all is taken of the objective value of the person, or of the objective laws and principles governing the co-habitation of persons of different sex.'

This combination of a union of persons and the procreative purpose ordained by nature results in a unique relationship. Wojtyla writes: 'Looked at objectively, the marital relationship is not therefore just a union of persons, a reciprocal relationship between a man and a woman, but is essentially a union of persons affected by the possibility of procreation.' He stresses the fact that marital relations may give life to a new person and for their union to be a full one it must be accompanied by the possibility that the man may become a father and the woman a mother. The union of persons, he stresses, is 'not the same as sexual union. This latter is raised to the level of the person only when it is accompanied in the mind and the will by the acceptance of the possibility of parenthood. It is the exclusion of this possibility of parenthood that renders contraception evil.'

On the other hand Wojtyla declares the rhythm method of birth control to be legitimate. 'They are merely adapting themselves to the laws of nature, to the order which reigns in nature. The fertility cycle in woman is part of that order. Nature makes procreation possible in the fertile period, and impossible in the infertile period. But deliberate prevention of procreation by human beings acting contrary to the order and the laws of nature is quite a different matter.'

It can thus be seen that the Pope's attitude to birth control rests on two bases: first, procreation must never be excluded totally from a marriage, but it may be excluded temporarily by use of 'natural' methods. Deliberate exclusion of the possibility of procreation conflicts not only with the order of nature but with love itself. It reduces the whole content of the marital act to sexual enjoyment and excludes a true union of man and woman on a personal level. The conclusions of Wojtyla rest upon an absolute distinction between natural and unnatural methods of birth control but he does not elaborate on this distinction nor attempt to establish it other than as a statement of fact. Yet it was precisely the inability to demonstrate the validity of this distinction which led the majority of the conciliar commission on birth control to come to the conclusion that artificial methods of birth control might be used in marriage provided they were used with a sense of responsibility and not wholly to frustrate its procreative purpose. A full discussion of the issues that are involved here can be found in Chapter IV of *Love and Responsibility*, 'Justice towards the Creator'. Wojtyla's argument from personalist grounds would I think be more convincing if it also excluded the use of the safe period as a means of birth control. (For a discussion of the issues involved see also my book *The Agonising Choice*, Eyre and Spottiswoode, 1971, especially Chapter VI, 'Theological Perspectives'.)

It is from this personalist viewpoint that divorce is ruled out; as are artificial methods of birth control; so is adultery; so are pre-marital sexual relations, and so is any form of 'sexual perversion'. All these are incompatible with the full self-giving of one person to another. It is only when one understands Wojtyla's commitment to this high personalist doctrine of marriage that one can understand his statement which aroused so much controversy and ridicule in October 1980 that there was a possibility of adultery within the bonds of marriage. The Pope then spoke of 'adultery in the heart' in marriage, and meant that it was possible within the marriage bond for the wife to be used as an object. (He did not, however, refer to the fact that such a possibility can also arise with the woman using the husband as an object.)

The Pope has further made it plain that his predecessors' condemnation of abortion is fully shared by him. This is hardly surprising in view of the unbroken tradition of condemnation of abortion in the Catholic Church from the earliest times until today. The Pope makes a clear distinction between birth control and abortion. Thus in *Love and Responsibility* Wojtyla writes: 'There are no grounds for discussing abortion in conjunction with birth control. To do so would be quite improper.' It would not only be improper but it would be highly dangerous. If abortion is presented merely as a variant of birth control then the struggle to convince the modern consciousness of the evil of abortion would be made virtually impossible. Artificial contraception is widely accepted, but the same is not true to the same extent of abortion. This corresponds to a real distinction—birth control lies within the sphere of sexual ethics whereas abortion concerns human rights.

Pope John Paul's condemnation of divorce stems from both personalist and social considerations. When in Ireland he went further than a moral condemnation of divorce and appeared to be suggesting that it should not be allowed by law at all: 'Divorce, for whatever reason it is introduced, inevitably becomes easier and easier to obtain, and it gradually comes to be accepted as a normal part of life. The very possibility of divorce in the sphere of civil law makes permanent and stable values more difficult for everyone. May Ireland always continue to give witness before the modern world to her traditional commitment to the sanctity and the indissolubility of the marriage bond. May the Irish always support marriage through . . . positive social and legal actions.' Here the Pope was treading on dangerous ground because he seems to have passed beyond the role of moral counsellor into the sphere of politics and legal action.

The Pope was not in fact so explicit as he had been in Ireland on another moral legal issue, which arose in Italy, namely the referendum held there on 17 May 1981, as to whether the reformed abortion law which had been in force for three years should be repealed. The Pope was careful not to mention the referendum itself but his constant condemnation of abortion during the period prior to the holding of the referendum was no doubt intended to influence Italian opinion. He was fully within his rights to do so, but he was severely criticized by a number of Italian politicians for interfering in the internal affairs of Italy. In the event, the referendum favoured legalized abortion and the papal interventions do not seem to have had great influence on the result. They may indeed have been counter-productive because of the strong feeling in modern Italy against interference by the Church in what are seen as political affairs.

CELIBACY

The Pope takes a lofty view of priesthood and expects high standards from priests. His attitude towards them is challenging and at times even harsh. From a number of his speeches it is clear that he regards the priesthood as a full-time totally committed ministry and is unsympathetic towards experiment and innovation. He regards the priest as a special witness to Christ in the community and perhaps for this reason approves of worker priests.

On celibacy, the Pope is adamant in upholding the tradition of the Western Church. Celibacy is, however, a matter of discipline rather than of doctrine. In apostolic times both priests and bishops were married and today the Eastern Church retains a married clergy though not a married episcopate. In the West, on the other hand, celibacy was fully established by the twelfth century and has been maintained ever since. The Pope gave a clear sign of his views in the first encyclical of his reign, *Redemptor Hominis*, which appeared in spring 1979 and in which celibacy was commended. On Maundy Thursday, 12 April 1979, the Pope issued a letter 'To all the priests of the Church' and made it clear that there was to be no relaxation of the celibacy rule.

The Pope conceded that the tradition of celibacy was peculiar to the Latin Church, but added that it was 'a tradition to which she owes much and in which she is resolved to persevere in spite of all the difficulties to which such fidelity

Nuns wait patiently for the Pope

could be exposed, and also in spite of the various symptoms of weakness and crisis in individual priests'. The Pope upheld celibacy not only as an eschatological sign but one of great social meaning in the service of the people of God. He denied that there was any invasion of human rights in the imposition of celibacy since the commitment is made in full awareness and freedom after training lasting a number of years and after reflection and prayer.

In this respect papal teaching does not seem to have changed since the Council of Trent in 1563 where canon 10 declared: 'If anyone says the married state excels the state of virginity or celibacy . . . let him be anathema.'

During his visit to Africa and again in Germany Pope John Paul stressed the importance of retaining celibacy. He disallowed the petition put forward by the Indonesian bishops for a married clergy and expressed a similar attitude towards such requests in South America. The Pope's stand on celibacy drew a sharp comment from Professor Hans Küng, who accused him of 'violating the human right to marriage within the Church while posing as a defender of human rights outside the Roman Catholic Church' (reported in the *Tablet*, 5 May 1979).

The Pope and the Church

The Pope has also set his face against any extension of the priesthood to women. In Philadelphia on 4 October 1979, he declared: 'The fact that there is a personal individual call to the priesthood given by the Lord to "the men he himself had decided upon" is in accord with the prophetic traditions. It should help us, too, to understand that the Church's traditional decision to call men to the priest-hood and not to call women is not a statement about human rights nor an exclusion of women from holiness and mission in the Church. Rather this decision expresses the conviction of the Church about this particular dimension of the gift of priesthood by which God has chosen to shepherd his flock.'

CLERICAL DRESS

Pope John Paul is a strong upholder of a distinctive clerical dress and will not countenance priests dressing in the same manner as the laity. Addressing priests at Maynooth during his visit to Ireland, he said: 'Rejoice to be witnesses to Christ in the modern world. . . . Do not help the trend towards "taking God off the streets" by adopting secular modes of dress and behaviour yourselves.' The Pope had put his own principles into practice when he first visited America as a cardinal, insisting that he and the bishops who accompanied him should dress throughout the tour in their cassocks with red buttons and trimmings. In Communist countries, of course, the cassock is a challenge to the regime, but when Cardinal Wojtyla appeared in it in New York the principal effect was to cause traffic jams!

LAICIZATION OF PRIESTS

More important than the question of clerical dress is that of laicization of priests. In recent years there has been an exodus from the priesthood resulting from the changes and disturbances brought about by the Second Vatican Council. In 1973, for example, 3,690 priests were laicized and the figure was still over 2,000 in 1978. One of the early acts of the Pope's pontificate was to stop the process of laicization, a step which caused considerable controversy and distress.

I had first-hand evidence of the distress, since I have been chairman for a number of years of a society, New Bearings, which exists to help nuns and priests in difficulty with their ministry. The society is still in existence today and deals with about fifty cases a year. Accordingly, when I was received in private audience by the Pope on 24 May 1980, I raised the question of the ban on laicization and explained the difficulties that it was causing.

I also suggested in a memorandum which I left with the Pope that there should be a new procedure by which the principal investigation and decision would be taken in the home country of the priest concerned, subject only to confirmation by Rome. The Pope responded immediately and told me that the way to laicization would be opened again. He explained that he had closed it because he felt that the process had become too 'legal' and insufficiently 'pastoral' or 'spiritual'. He explained that the matter was being considered by the Holy Office and that a decision would not long be delayed. I was extremely grateful for this forthcoming attitude on the part of the Pope and he was as good as his word. A few months later the process of laicization started up again and new norms were issued.

Though these norms were highly secret they were in fact published in the *Tablet* for 29 November 1980. They made it clear that ordination once conferred cannot be annulled but the 'validity' may be challenged on grounds of duress or defective intention at the time of ordination. The cases to be considered are: 'Those who should not have received priestly ordination because the necessary aspect of freedom of responsibility was lacking or because the competent superiors were not within an appropriate time able to judge in a prudent and sufficiently fitting way whether the candidate really was suited for continuously leading a life of celibacy dedicated to God.' It can be seen that the norms do not allow laicization in a situation where a priest has simply lost his vocation and wishes to return to the lay state, or wishes to enter the matrimonial state, groups which in my experience constitute by far the majority of cases. The grounds of laicization are similar to those allowed for the nullity of marriage. The two situations, however, are not parallel, for a lifelong commitment is of the essence of marriage, whereas it cannot be argued that a commitment to celibacy is of the essence of priesthood.

The local bishop is to conduct the inquiry into the case and it is for him to decide whether there is sufficient evidence for the case to be forwarded to Rome. In Rome, the issues and the evidence are to be considered by the Holy Office who will then present the case for laicization to the pope, or reject it, or request that more evidence should be submitted. In each case the final decision will be that of the pope himself. Whether this procedure will prove adequate for the complexity of the cases with which it will have to deal, remains to be seen, but it is certainly an improvement that the process should have been opened again. There is believed to be a backlog of about 4,000 cases where priests are seeking laicization, and a trickle of dispensations has begun to come through.

THE POPE AND THE JESUITS

Jesuits have traditionally been the papal right-hand men but in recent years have grown somewhat apart from the Vatican. The Pope is known to be concerned

Altar boys, Germany 1980

about what he sees as the politicizing of the South American Jesuits and the secularizing of their counterparts in the United States. After the illness of the Father General, Padre Arrupe, the Pope vetoed the election of a new General and put in his own nominee as Vicar General, the 80-year-old conservative, Fr Dezza. The purpose of this manoeuvre was to enable Fr Dezza to make provincial appointments of men with the Pope's own outlook who in due course would elect a Father General of like mind. This move has caused sharp controversy inside and outside the order.

THE POPE AND THE DISSIDENTS

Pope John Paul was elected in part to bring an effective stabilizing influence back into the Church after the upheavals and excitements of the past two decades. There is no doubt that the College of Cardinals elected him in the hope that he would curb theological and liturgical 'excesses' and reassert once again 'the great discipline' of the Church. In this he has so far been remarkably successful. He has tackled firmly the issues raised by the theologians Professor Hans Küng and Father Schillebeeckx, called the Dutch bishops to Rome for a special synod to reconcile their differences and strengthen their links with the Holy See, and opened the way for the return of Archbishop Lefebvre, the conservative rebel, to the fold. The Pope's actions have been criticized by liberal Catholics and fears have been expressed that a conservative reaction is taking place, but the papal interventions have more the character of a restoring of a balance than of a brutal repression. There has been nothing like the ruthless campaign waged against the Modernists during the pontificate of Pius X.

THE CASE OF HANS KÜNG

Professor Hans Küng, one of the most brilliant and outspoken of contemporary Catholic popular theologians, had been in trouble with the Holy Office in Rome long before John Paul II came to the papal throne. His books *The Church* (1967) and *Infallible?* (1971) were both suspected by Roman theologians of containing heretical tendencies.

The essence of the Küng approach to infallibility was to elevate the idea of indefectibility in the Church to a position of such prominence that it would overshadow the actual doctrinal definition of papal infallibility of the First Vatican Council. Father Küng was soon in difficulties with his own bishops in

Germany, who in February 1971 issued a statement accusing him of departing from certain fundamental elements of Catholic orthodoxy. Five months later in July 1971 the Holy Office followed up with a list of theses culled from *Infallible?* which they maintained were irreconcilable with Catholic doctrine.

Küng was required to submit a reply within thirty days. He eventually did reply but vigorously defended himself and his objectives: 'What I am aiming at is a Church that, acting in the spirit of the gospel of Jesus Christ, does much more than hitherto for the men and women of today and for their anxieties and needs.' The struggle, since it can hardly be called a dialogue, between Father Küng and the Holy Office continued, culminating in the issue in July 1973 of a document by the Holy Office entitled *Mysterium Ecclesiae*. Father Küng was not specifically mentioned but it was aimed principally against his views. Eventually he was given a choice either to accept the declaration or to come to Rome for a discussion with the Holy Office theologians.

Father Küng would not agree unless conditions he had laid down as far back as 1968 were accepted, namely that he would have the right to see the dossier the Holy Office had compiled on himself, that he would have the right to appoint his own counsel to defend him and not have to accept an appointee of the Office, that he would be informed of his rights of appeal and that a decision would be reached within a set time limit. Such conditions are familiar enough to the English common law but are not so well known to Roman canonists. They were not agreed to by the Holy Office and as a consequence Küng never made the journey to the eternal city. Despite this impasse, the battle was not fought to the death and after a protracted correspondence Küng conceded in September 1974 that he did not exclude the possibility that his views and those of the *magisterium* would eventually come into harmony. The Holy Office's response to this somewhat leafless olive branch was to bring the proceedings against his two books to an end.

Peace thus appeared to have been established, but war broke out again with the publication of *On Being a Christian* (1977). This book, which became a best seller, dealt with the divinity of Jesus and the nature of the resurrection in a manner which was found highly unsatisfactory by traditional theologians. The controversy became more bitter than that generated by *Infallible?*, for it was felt that more fundamental issues were at stake, which went to the heart of the Christian faith.

Professor Küng's own purpose was, he declared, that of de-mythologizing. He maintained: 'It is undeniable that, in generally current ideas of Christianity, Jesus Christ is often thought of, more or less, as a God descending to earth whose humanity is basically only a kind of clothing behind which God himself speaks and acts.' This defence did not disarm the German bishops and a number of theologians who continued to be critical. A dialogue intended to resolve differences took place between Küng and his critics on 22 January 1977 at Stuttgart. This was followed by an effort by Cardinal Höffner to get Küng to answer some categorical questions, such as, 'Is Jesus Christ the uncreated, eternal son of God, consubstantial with the Father?' Küng, however, declined to be made the subject of what he considered an over simplified inquisition. Eventually he confirmed that he did accept the formula of the Council of Chalcedon, of 'truly God and truly man', but added that what was important for him was that this formulation should be understood correctly.

Pope Paul, who was then reigning, did not wish to bring matters to a head and appears to have been following a policy of spinning out time in the hope that some accommodation would be reached. That was the situation at his death.

With the accession of Pope John Paul II an alteration came about in the attitude of the Holy Office. Matters were pursued with greater urgency and there was a distinct change of policy. For example, in September 1979, the French Dominican Father Jacques Pohier fell under a papal ban for allegedly denying the bodily resurrection of Christ in his book *Quand je dis Dieu*. Again, Father Schillebeeckx was summoned to Rome in the autumn of 1979 to justify the views he had put forward in his book *Jesus: An Experiment in Christology*.

The atmosphere was thus already threatening when Father Küng gave an appraisal of the Pope's first year in office. This appeared originally on 13 October 1979 in the *Frankfurter Allgemeine Zeitung* and later in *Le Monde* and the *New York Times* as well. In the starkest terms, Küng raised some of the questions troubling liberal Catholics about developments in the new papal reign. 'Is the commitment in the Church to human rights in the world honest, when in the Church itself, at the same time, human rights are not fully guaranteed—for example, the right of priests to marry, as is guaranteed in the gospel itself and in the old Catholic tradition; the right to leave the priesthood with an official dispensation after a thorough examination of conscience (rather than the inhumane practice re-introduced by this Pope of forbidding bureaucratically dispensation); the right of theologians to freedom in their research and expression of opinion; the right of nuns to choose their own clothing; the ordination of women, as can certainly be justified by the gospel for our contemporary situation; the personal responsibility of married couples for the conception and the number of their children?'

This was coat trailing with a vengeance and the article was not received rapturously in Rome, but the trigger that led to his condemnation seems to have been not so much the article but the foreword he wrote to a book by another German theologian, August Hasler, dealing with Piux IX, the First Vatican Council and the definition of infallibility. In the book, Pio Nono is represented as dotty and unbalanced, and those pressing for the definition of infallibility as unscrupulous conspirators. Hasler even suggested that Pio Nono was the father of Cardinal Guidi, with whom he had a dispute over the definition! The ire of Rome was aroused but Father Hasler cheated the Holy Office by dying and passing before a higher tribunal. Hans Küng was left behind.

No doubt Father Küng was wholly sincere in wanting to discuss again the whole problem of infallibility, and a problem it remains. In Father Küng's view the situation today in relation to infallibility is similar to that of the temporal power at the time of Pio Nono. He urged John Paul to do something about it, and this was reasonable enough, but to write a commendatory foreword to the somewhat scurrilous Hasler book was possibly not the best way of going about it. This time Küng had gone too far and on 18 December 1979 the Holy Office issued a statement declaring 'that in his writing Professor Hans Küng departs from the integral truth of the Catholic faith and that therefore he cannot be regarded as a Catholic theologian nor perform the task of teaching as one'. His licence to teach as an official Catholic theologian of the Church was withdrawn. Curiously enough the Holy Office seems to have been more concerned with his views on infallibility than with his Christology.

Inevitably there were widespread protests among theologians and others at the punishment which had been meted out to Father Küng. Many feared that it was the beginning of the end of freedom of inquiry in the Church, and others were anxious about its damaging effect on the ecumenical movement. There is no doubt that the Pope personally approved of the decision and on his side it could be argued that he was acting in accordance with the practice of collegiality, since the German bishops had been specifically pressing for an exercise of papal power. He might also claim that he had been severely provoked. Professor Küng was unable to continue holding his chair of theology at Tübingen University, and a long and expensive legal battle over the interpretation of academic freedom and the concordat between Germany and the Vatican might have ensued. However, the difficulty was overcome by supplying him with another chair at Tübingen but outside the theological faculty as such.

The effect of the papal intervention appears to have been limited. Father Küng has not been silenced nor even greatly inconvenienced. His lectures continue and at the end of 1980 he wrote another open letter to the Pope, backed up this time by 135 German theologians. In a letter to the German bishops of May 1980, Pope John Paul upheld the doctrine of papal infallibility but left the way open to a reconciliation: 'I would like to repeat to him [Hans Küng] what has already been said in other circumstances: we continue to nourish the hope that such agreement about the truth proclaimed and professed by the Church may eventually be reached that he might once again be able to be called a "Catholic theologian"; this title necessarily presupposes the authentic faith of the Church and a readiness to serve her mission in the manner clearly defined and realized over the centuries.' (*The Tablet*, 31 May 1980)

FATHER SCHILLEBEECKX

Perhaps even more serious than the clash between the Holy Office and Father Küng was that involving Father Schillebeeckx who was summoned to Rome in November 1979 to defend his book *Jesus: An Experiment in Christology*. He had long been engaged in Christological studies, the fruits of which were to be published in three volumes, *Jesus: An Experiment in Christology* (Collins, 1979) and *Christ: The Christian Experience in the Modern World* (SCM Press, 1980). The final volume of the trilogy has not yet been published. Although not as well known as Father Küng, Father Schillebeeckx is considered one of the leading theologians in the Catholic Church and was one of the architects of the Second Vatican Council. He had been in trouble before with the Holy Office in 1968, but the attack had subsided after Professor Karl Rahner had rallied to his defence. A list of theological questions was put to him in late 1979 and he did agree to go to Rome.

Meanwhile, the Faculty of Theology of Louvain University passed a motion expressing their full support for Father Schillebeeckx. In December 1980 the Holy Office issued their conclusions which had received the approval of the Pope. The Holy Office took note of the clarifications that had been made by Father Schillebeeckx, but considered there were certain points where the explanations given were not sufficient to remove the ambiguities. Cardinal Seper, the Prefect of the Holy Office, concluded his letter with these words: 'I would be grateful if you would let me know what means you would feel it would be best to take to satisfy the requests I have made. The Congregation itself would be thinking in terms of an article prepared by you in agreement with it, taking the document accompanying the present letter as a guide. But it is prepared to consider any other means you would propose.'

At a press conference in Nijmegen on 4 December, Father Schillebeeckx made it clear that he had no intention of publishing any new statement or article. He felt that the disputed points in the first two volumes of his book had been dealt with and the third volume would cover the disputed issue of the authority of the *magisterium*. In his view the Holy Office wanted him to use 'the classical dogmatic formulas' and this he declined to do: 'because they are not accessible to contemporary man'.

THE DUTCH CHURCH

Perhaps the most difficult of the 'dissident problems' tackled by Pope John Paul was that of the Dutch Church. Since the sixties the Vatican had been plagued by what was little less than a revolution in Dutch Catholicism which changed that Church from one of the most conservative in Europe into one of the most progressive. Democratic structures were adopted and a national pastoral council set up, with advisory though not executive functions. This council promptly recommended that celibacy should not be required for ordination to the priesthood and that marriage should be an option available to priests. Traditional seminaries were closed and candidates for the priesthood sent to theological faculties at the universities. The Dutch bishops decided to leave the question of contraception to the consciences of the faithful, a new catechism was adopted, widespread and various liturgical experimentation took place.

In an effort to check these 'excesses' the Vatican appointed two highly conservative bishops, Monsignor Simonis and Monsignor Gijsens, to the vacant Sees of Rotterdam and Roermond. These appointments merely exacerbated the situation and the new bishops found themselves at loggerheads with the Primate, Cardinal Willebrands, and the other four Dutch bishops, as well as with the leaders of the Dutch religious orders. Although things were allowed to drift on during the last years of the reign of Pope Paul, it was clear that this could not continue indefinitely without the Dutch Church either lapsing into chaos or moving into schism.

Accordingly Pope John Paul took the initiative, and summoned the Dutch bishops to Rome for a special synod in January 1980. The synod provided a remarkably good example of both the Pope's strength and his flexibility. By joining the Dutch bishops to himself he gave an example of collegiality in practice. Although he did not intervene in the synod he was present at all the sessions, listening carefully throughout, and for a period of over two weeks made himself part of the bishops' lives. Seven cardinals—Cardinal Willebrands and six curial prelates—took part in the proceedings, but the dominating personality was that of the Pope. His presence resulted in the creation of a real unity. The purpose of the synod was to end the division between the bishops, to establish a new framework of orthodoxy and to improve communications with Rome. In all these ends the synod proved successful. The most conservative of the bishops, Bishop Gijsens of Roermond, was brought to heel and undertook to co-operate with his fellow prelates. All the Dutch bishops, the cardinals and the Pope himself, subscribed to a solemn document issued at the end of the synod which contained a number of important and basic propositions.

First, the bishops expressed their unanimous wish to increase cordial and fraternal relations among themselves. They declared their agreement with the content of the Catholic faith according to the teaching of the Roman Catholic Church. They declared, too, that neither they nor their priests were delegates of the laity but were ministers of Jesus Christ at the service of the ecclesial community. They then went on to undertake to preach the content of revelation as interpreted by the *magisterium* while taking into account the requirements of modern conditions. The bishops acknowledged there was a *sensus fidei*, a grasp of the faith, which belonged to the people, but distinguished this from revelation. The declaration went on to make clear that a distinction existed between the ministerial or sacramental priesthood and the priesthood common to all the baptized. They declared their belief in the importance of the spiritual life, of the divine office, of daily celebration of the mass, of the sacrament of penance and of spiritual dialogue. They recognized that celibacy constituted a great good for the Church and promised to follow faithfully the decisions of the Pope to maintain the celibate rules. They also agreed to supplement the teaching of theology in the universities by the setting up of genuine seminaries. As for ecumenism, the bishops agreed that inter-communion between Catholics and the separated brethren was not the appropriate response to Christ's call for unity.

In addition to these theological declarations, the bishops agreed to certain practical steps. Full information was to be exchanged at regular intervals with Vatican officials. At the same time any accusations or information about the state of the Dutch Church sent to Rome were to be verified through consultation with the appropriate bishop. The bishops agreed to study 'possibilities for new diocesan boundaries in their country, not necessarily to be realized en bloc'. The significance of this was the proposition from the Vatican that there should be three new bishoprics set up in Holland, and the fear of many Dutch Catholics that the opportunity would be taken to appoint new conservative prelates. It was also agreed that a synodal council made up of the Dutch bishops and a representative of the Pope should be formed to see that the conclusions were put into practice. Two other commissions were to be established: one to study the ways in which lay people could take part in the pastoral work of the Church and the other to ensure satisfactory arrangements were being made for the education of candidates for the priesthood.

Thus the saga of the Dutch Church was given a new turn and a new chapter opened. In February of the following year the Pope expressed the wish that there should be a follow-up to see how the synod's conclusions had been carried out in practice. There can be no doubting of the Pope's firmness in his handling of the synod and the problems of the Dutch Church, but at the same time the bishops were not faced with impossible or peremptory demands. What practical effects the synod will have on the Church in Holland remains to be seen.

ARCHBISHOP LEFEBVRE

Plagued on the one hand by Catholic liberals, Pope John Paul has also had to deal with Catholic conservatives, notably Archbishop Lefebvre. In some ways the Archbishop's views, particularly on celibacy, priestly discipline and the wearing of clerical dress, are calculated to appeal to the Pope. On the other hand he would have no sympathy with the Archbishop's total rejection of the Second Vatican Council and its documents. The Archbishop could hardly have made matters plainer than in his declaration of faith of 21 November 1974 in which he said: 'We refuse to follow the Rome of neo-modernist and neo-protestant tendencies which clearly manifested themselves in the Second Council, and after the Council in the reforms which ensued from it. . . . it is impossible for any conscious and faithful Catholic to adopt this reform and to submit to it in any way whatever.'

One can see from this statement that the Archbishop's quarrel with the Church goes far beyond the issue of whether the Tridentine mass should be celebrated or not. Furthermore, he has set up his own seminary illegally at Ecône, in Switzerland, and despite prohibitions from the Vatican has continued to conduct ordinations. In 1976 the Archbishop was suspended by the Vatican *'a divinis'*, which meant that he could no longer function legitimately as a bishop. Thus things continued until the death of Pope Paul, but with the election of the present Pope there came signs of a thaw.

On 21 January 1979, the Archbishop, preaching a sermon at Caen, in Normandy, declared that he recognized that 'the atmosphere at the Vatican has changed' and that he was no longer confronted 'with men who have decided to condemn me before even hearing what I have to say', but with those 'who know there is a master above them who wishes the matter to be settled'. Earlier in January, Archbishop Lefebvre had visited the Holy Office in Rome for conversations with its Prefect, Cardinal Seper, and other members of the congregation. The Holy Office is now considering the whole case, and when this has been done a dossier will be compiled and submitted first to the cardinals who are attached to the Holy Office, and finally to the Pope, who will have to pronounce on Lefebvre's case. In 1980 an exchange of letters took place between Cardinal Seper and the Archbishop, and conditions for lifting the suspension were discussed. There is some optimism that a reconciliation will be brought about. *Videbimus!*

THE GOVERNMENT OF THE CHURCH

Immediately after his election and on a number of occasions since, Pope John Paul has declared his support for the idea of collegiality, the system by which the Church is governed by the college of bishops with the Pope at its head.

He has been scrupulous to consult with the bishops of each country he has

At Fulda Cathedral, Germany 1980

visited before setting off on his travels. The high points in all the countries visited have been the meetings with and the addresses to the bishops' conferences. This has been a notable, if unforeseen example of collegiality in practice. The Pope has also been careful in the case of the Dutch Church and in the disputes over Professor Hans Küng to act in full co-operation with the bishops concerned.

In November 1979, for the first time in 400 years, he called a meeting of the College of Cardinals to discuss Vatican finances, but no details of their conclusions nor of the finances themselves were revealed. There have, however, been no efforts to develop collegial institutions further in the Church. The synod of bishops of the whole Church met in Rome 1980 to discuss the family, but it has remained a consultative body and no effort has been made to develop any executive powers.

This synod on 'The role of the Christian family in the modern world', which opened in Rome on 26 September 1980 and lasted four weeks, provides the best example of how the idea of collegiality is working in practice. More than 200 cardinals and bishops took part in the deliberations and reported frankly on the situation in their individual countries. This part of the synod was generally considered to have been valuable. First of all there was a positive approach to questions of sexuality and marriage. A typical contribution came from Cardinal Hume on the evening of 29 September, when he pointed out that husbands and wives had a particular prophetic mission, based on their experience as married persons, to contribute authoritatively to discussion of marital problems: 'This experience and this understanding constitute, I would suggest, an authentic *fons theologica* from which we, the pastors and indeed the whole Church, can draw.'

A principle of 'gradualness' emerged from the discussions, indicating that the full rigours of the law could not be applied all at once and in every case without regard to individual and local circumstances. *Humanae Vitae* and the question of birth control were fully discussed and it was made clear, notably by the Archbishop of San Francisco, that there was still considerable opposition to the conclusions of the encyclical. Cardinal Hume also contributed to this debate, pointing out that there were couples for whom natural methods of birth control did not commend themselves as the only solution: 'It cannot just be said that these persons have failed to overcome their human frailty and weakness. Indeed, such persons are often good, conscientious and faithful sons and daughters of the Church. They just cannot accept that the use of artificial means of contraception in some circumstances is *intrinsice inhonestum*, as this latter has been generally understood.' This contrasted strongly with Cardinal Ratzinger's declaration at the opening of the synod when he condemned artificial means of contraception, saying: 'By using chemical means to manipulate the natural rhythm of reproduction, man dangerously oversteps the limits of his activity *vis à vis* nature. There is therefore a growing awareness of the need to respect nature in the biological domain.'

The question of the admission of divorced persons who had remarried to the sacraments was also discussed, notably by Archbishop Worlock of Liverpool. He raised two pertinent questions: 'Is this spirit of repentance and desire for sacramental strength to be forever frustrated? Can they be told only that they must reject their new responsibilities as a necessary condition for forgiveness and restoration to sacramental life?' The issue of women's rights was also discussed and particular problems rising from marital conditions in countries such as Africa. In all, the synod put forward forty-three propositions on which the prelates voted. But none of the propositions nor the voting figures were officially published, though they have since appeared 'unofficially' in the *Tablet*. They were submitted to the Pope who had been present for a large part of the synod, although once again he did not take part in the discussions.

At the conclusion of the synod a message was sent by the bishops to the families of the world. This message reaffirmed the permanence and indissolubility of sacramental marriage, upheld the rejection of contraception by the encyclical *Humanae Vitae*, and condemned both sterilization and abortion. The Pope when he came to give his final address to the synod also upheld the teaching of the encyclical and reaffirmed the traditional teaching of the Church that divorced people who had married again could only be admitted to the sacraments if they abstained from all acts of sexual intercourse. He also had some critical remarks to make about the concept of gradualness: 'In fact the "law of gradualness", as it is called, is not possible unless a person sincerely obeys the divine law and seeks those benefits that are protected and promoted by that law. For the law of gradualness (or gradual progress) cannot be the same as "gradualness of the law" as if there were various grades or forms of commandment for different men and circumstances in the divine law.' He also made it plain that women should not be obliged by social conditions to work outside the home.

What is one to make of the synod, seen as a manifestation of collegiality? The answer must be that it was extremely disappointing. The call for openness of information made by Bishop Agnellus Andrew at the opening of the synod was hardly upheld by insisting on a total blanket of secrecy on the resolutions put forward. Moreover, the Pope himself does not seem to have been even marginally influenced by the discussions, and in his closing address reaffirmed attitudes which had already become wholly familiar through the addresses made on his travels throughout the world. After this latest example of the synod's work in practice, as disappointing as the previous two sessions, the future usefulness of the synod as a body must be seriously in doubt.

The Pope and the Church

THE POPE'S SOCIAL TEACHING

Since the time of Leo XIII the popes have been active in developing a social doctrine of the Church. Pope Leo himself published the encyclical *Rerum Novarum* in 1891 and this was followed by Pius XI's *Quadragesimo Anno* in 1931. These documents ranged the Catholic Church firmly on the side of the movements for social and industrial reform. Pope John Paul II was working on an encyclical to commemorate the ninetieth anniversary of *Rerum Novarum* when he was gunned down in St Peter's Square, but the letter was completed and issued in September 1981, under the title *Laborem Exercens* (*On Human Work*, Vatican Polyglot Press, Rome 1981).

Pope John Paul may be theologically conservative, but his new encyclical on work shows that he is a sharp critic of the economic systems of the western world. The encyclical opens with a resounding declaration of man's right to work—a right which springs from a fundamental human need. The opportunity to work is essential for the dignity of man. Unemployment, which he defines as 'the lack of work for those who are capable of it', is both an evil and an injustice and it is the duty of government to counter it by overall planning. He gives a clear warning that if these needs are not met then social disorder and violence are likely to result.

On wider social and economic issues the Holy Father has no time for the views of theorists such as Professor Hayek and Sir Keith Joseph. Unrestrained capitalism is not a just social system and the Pope enunciates 'the principle of the priority of labour over capital', insisting that capitalism must be made to serve human values. True, the Pope upholds the right to private property but not as an absolute: goods are held in trust for others as well as oneself: and nationalization may well be the right solution in particular cases.

The articulation of such general principles will undoubtedly have long-term influence, but the section of the encyclical most likely to make immediate impact is that on trade unions. With the fate of Poland's national trade union Solidarity, and therefore of Polish independence, hanging in the balance, the Pope has come to the aid of his fellow countrymen and thrown the weight of his spiritual office behind their demands. In June 1981 he received Mr Walesa and other Polish trade union leaders, and said that he hoped they would be able to continue their work with courage, prudence and moderation. The Pope declares the inalienable right of the Poles to organize themselves into unions to defend their interests. Unions, he declares, are an intrinsic part of the struggle for social justice and the achievement of the rights of working people. There is no doubt, says the Pope, that workers have the right to strike, but he warns that the weapon is one of the last not first resort. In an interesting passage he declares that unions should confine themselves to their industrial role and not be

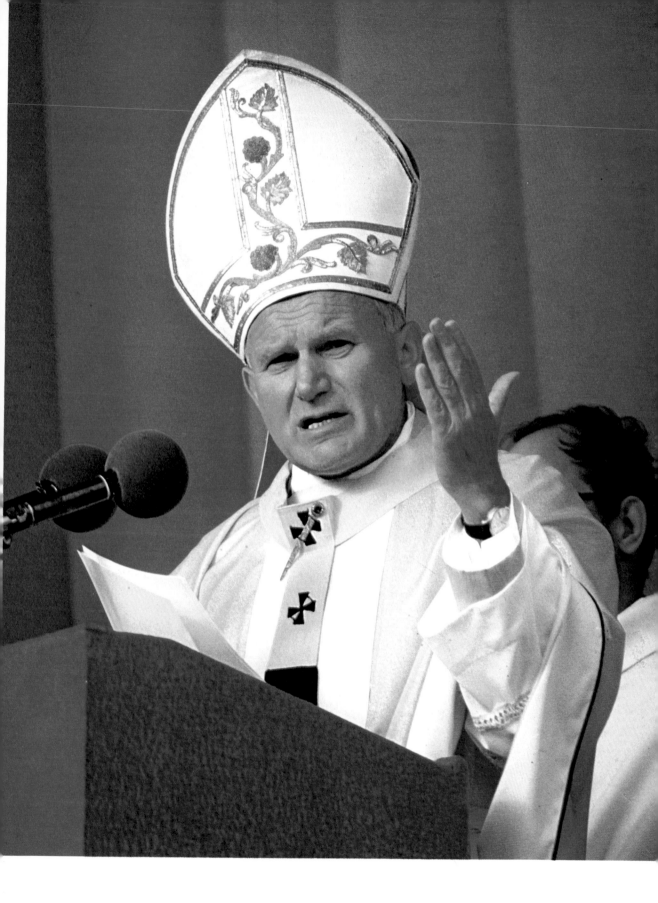

'subjected to the decisions of political parties or have too close links with them'. If they allow this to happen they will be distracted from their true ends and be used for political purposes.

The Pope goes on to make a number of practical suggestions to be applied in the economic sphere. He is greatly concerned about the increase in youth unemployment and counsels that the educational system should be geared to the world of work. Pope John Paul wants either a family wage or a generous system of family allowances so that women will not be forced to go out to work if they wish to remain at home and look after their families.

But it is to the 'gospel of work' that the Pope again and again returns: 'Just as human activity proceeds from man, so it is ordered towards man. For when a man works he not only alters things and society, he develops himself as well. He learns much, he cultivates his resources, he goes outside of himself and beyond himself. Rightly understood this kind of growth is of greater value than external riches.'

THE POPE AS BISHOP OF ROME

The Pope is not Bishop of Rome because he is Pope, but he is Pope because he is Bishop of Rome. Despite this close connection between the Pope and the eternal city, most popes in modern times, with the notable exception of Pope John, have been content to delegate their local episcopal powers to others. The present Pope has reversed this practice and plays an active part in his own diocese. At regular intervals, and always on a Sunday evening, the papal Mercedes issues forth from the Vatican carrying His Holiness on one of his pastoral visits to the 292 parishes of Rome. These visits are always well prepared in advance and are much more than public relations exercises. The Pope sees the church and the parish for himself, he meets the leading parishioners and often stays on to have a meal with the parish priest and the curates and discuss their problems.

Certainly the city of Rome faces immense ecclesiastical difficulties and challenges. There are only just over 1,100 priests in Rome for a population of 3 million people, and the city produces only a handful of ordinations a year. The population has grown at an extraordinary pace and is sprawled in concrete jungles outside the city walls. Every conceivable urban problem ranging from delinquency to drug addiction is being faced in this Roman subtopia. Of course, it would be beyond the capabilities of even this energetic pope to tackle all these issues, but he is undoubtedly making an impact upon them and the accusation cannot be levelled against him that while he is adept at solving other people's problems and advising them, he is neglecting his own diocese in Rome.

6

Portrait of a Pope

———— ✵ ————

Karol Wojtyla is probably the most extraordinary man ever to have been elected to the See of Peter. There are no parallels and no precursors. His election constituted a whole series of firsts: the first non-Italian pope for 400 years, the first pope to have come from Poland, the first pope to have emerged from behind the iron curtain.

These are the external events but Karol Wojtyla's character and personality appear equally unique. Popes have come from a wide variety of backgrounds but this is the first pope who has worked in a stone quarry, been trained as an actor, and tried his hand at being a poet. He is also a moral theologian, a philosopher and a mystic. Warm and outgoing to the crowds, they are moved by the beauty of his appearance but also seem to sense his holiness. In private he is much more contained—even a little withdrawn; an introvert more than an extrovert he is prepared to listen, although he gives no clue as to the effects that the words of his interlocutor may be having. He is a humble man, aware of the importance and grandeur of his position but keeping it in proportion and perspective by his sense of the greatness of the Master whom he serves.

POPE JOHN PAUL'S PRESENCE

Pope John Paul's presence is both majestic and electrifying. He radiates authority and strength: behind the soft folds of the papal robes are the real muscles of an athlete, formed in hiking, skiing and mountaineering. He has a military bearing but also a slight stoop. His head is handsome and his expression benevolent—he has a holy face. His countenance is open but bears the marks of suffering and endurance, much more markedly since the assassination attempt. His eyes are clear and blue.

The crowds gather, Germany 1980

Pope John Paul has a way with crowds and is helped by his perfect sense of timing. He gives them what they need and want: attention and concern. His smile is warm and cheering. No doubt all this reflects the training in his youth as an amateur actor. He speaks to crowds through gestures, by picking up a baby or embracing a prelate or greeting a pilgrim with recognition and warmth. In the age of television this is an invaluable quality.

The voice is a musical baritone, strong and resolute. His staff often hear it coming from his rooms when he is singing to himself the Polish tunes and hymns which he loves. The Pope has that indefinable thing, star quality, and what better setting could there be for its display than the eternal city? Rome is above all a theatrical city—a series of stage-sets mounting to the climax of the great semicircular auditorium ringed by Bernini's colonnade. In the Pope, it has found a personality worthy of its drama. He appeals to all ages but has a special appeal to youth. It is as though he has a particular message to give them, and they respond with rapture as they did in both Poland and Ireland. 'They see him as a man who lives the values behind the words,' said Bishop Casey of Galway.

Pope John Paul has an impish sense of humour which both attracts and disarms. It comes through when he is speaking to the crowds. He told them on one occasion that they should go home since it was time for their lunch and added, 'and that of the Pope'. On Easter Day 1979, he apologized for speaking in Polish, 'the only language I really know'. Sometimes he ends an address with homely words such as, 'Goodnight, see you tomorrow.' At Castel Gandolfo, an enthusiastic Italian was bellowing at him: 'Viva il Papa.' 'I wish I had a voice like that,' commented the Pope, 'I could use it in my job.' At Czestochowa when the crowds were singing that they wished him a hundred years of life, he replied that they would be better employed in wishing that his voice would last to the end of his visit. When arguing with officials about installing his swimming pool in Castel Gandolfo, a project in which he finally got his way, he commented, 'It's cheaper than another conclave.' After the assassination attempt by a Turk in St Peter's Square he was even able to quip that he had better go to Turkey again.

THE POPE'S PERSONALITY

Behind this brilliant façade lies a complex and gifted personality. Pope John Paul has a formidable intellect. He is a philosopher in his own right and his books are clear and closely argued. He is also prolific and his most recent bibliography (*The Mind of John Paul II: Origins of His Thought and Action*, George Hunston Williams, Seabury Press, New York, 1980) lists 630 items. His capacity for analysis of problems and issues is attested by those who have worked with him.

The only gap in his knowledge seems to be a scientific one—here he has no special expertise.

All popes claim to be linguists but not all live up to their claims. I remember an audience I once had with Pius XII, who was credited with fluency in English. I shall never forget the remark he made when I told him I was an undergraduate from Oxford. 'Ah,' cried the Pope in Pavlovian fashion, 'Oxford, Oxford, I have the great dictionary from Oxford.' Pope John Paul really does have the gift of tongues. He is fluent in Latin, French, German, Spanish and Italian, and at home in English, which he speaks idiomatically. Throughout my audiences with him, English has been the language spoken. Although at ease in a variety of languages, he finds speaking in foreign languages tiring at times and prefers his native Polish.

The Pope is very much a man of prayer. He is interested in mystical theology and has studied the writings and poems of St John of the Cross. His commitment to the Lord is shown in the motto he has chosen as his own, *Totius Tuus*. He is faithful to old friends and never forgets past favours, but he does not have close friendships. Long before he became pope he saw himself as a man apart, as an intrinsic element of his priesthood. Emotional personal involvements would strike him as unsuitable for a priest. Yet he is very human; he likes his food, particularly if it is Polish. On his flight to Ireland the Aer Lingus stewardess, who brought him the traditional Irish breakfast of eggs, bacon and black pudding, was impressed by the way he disposed of it: 'He's cleared his plate,' she said admiringly to her colleagues when she had removed the dishes.

THE POPE AS POET

Poetry plays an important part in the life of the Pope, as it does in those of so many of his fellow countrymen; but he is more than a lover of poetry, he is a poet in his own right. To be a poet and a pope seems at first a strange combination, but is it in fact such an odd conjunction? As Bagehot wrote, poetry is 'a deep thing, a teaching thing, the most surely and wisely elevating of human things'. And it was Wordsworth who proclaimed: 'Every great poet is a teacher: I wish either to be considered as a teacher, or as nothing.' Poetry is not only a 'teaching thing', it is a holy thing; it has a consecrating power and one would expect a man who is a mystic to have an interest in poetry as well. There is nothing intrinsically contradictory between being a poet and a priest—but, as Gerard Manley Hopkins knew, if the vocations in practice come into conflict, the priesthood has to come first. The Pope accepts this. In a foreword to an anthology of poetry written by priests and published in London in 1971, *Words in the Wilderness*, the then Cardinal Wojtyla wrote, 'Poetry has its own

significance, its own aesthetic value and criteria of appreciation which belong to its proper order. And that is what the authors included here are concerned about. But doubtless they are also concerned with making a point about their religious vocation. And very many of those who will read these poems may ask themselves questions regarding the mutual relationship of priesthood and poetry writing. Priesthood is a sacrament and vocation, while writing poetry is the function of talent; but it is talent too that determines the vocation.' I interpret these somewhat enigmatic words to mean that poetry and priesthood can in theory be harmoniously combined but that there may be practical difficulties. In effect for the Pope, poetry has been taken up into his priestly vocation and continues increasingly so. His later poems are meditations upon his religious views.

The papal poetry is of course Polish, a literary form which is syllabic rather than stressed in the English manner. The Pope's poems are marked more by assonance than by rhymes and are based on ideas rather than images, although they contain some striking ones. His poetry, as all poetry must be, is intensely personal and he published it under a protective pseudonym—only when he became pope was the anonymity stripped away. His choice of pseudonym was significant, Andrzej Jawien, the root of the last name signifying someone realizing himself and coming to the light.

The poetry spans three decades, from the mid-1940s to 1975. In 1946 came the first seventeen shorter poems. In 1950 he published *Song of the Brightness of Water*, a poem about Christ and the Samaritan woman whom he met at the well. In the same year came his poem *Mother*, inspired by Pius XII's definition of the dogma of the Assumption of the Virgin. In the late fifties he published *The Quarry* and *Profiles of a Cyrenean*. In the 1960s came *Easter Vigil*. Wojtyla seems to have been influenced in his own composition of poetry by the poems of St John of the Cross and those of the Polish poet Cyprian Norwid (1821–83).

The themes in Wojtyla's poetry form an interface with the ideas expressed by the Pope in his encyclicals and addresses, but because they are in poetic form their impact is both more powerful and more universal. Thus in his play *In Front of the Jeweller's Shop*, he sets out the idea of love which so influenced his first encyclical *Redemptor Hominis*: 'Every person has at his or her disposal an existence, and a love. The problem is: how to build a sensible structure out of it? This structure must never be inward looking. It must be open in such a way that, on the one hand, it embraces other people, on the other, it reflects absolute Existence and Love in some way, at all times.'

Work and man's struggle to impose his will on matter is the subject of Wojtyla's poem *The Quarry*:

Portrait of a Pope

Hands are a landscape. When they split, the pain of
*   their sores surges free as a stream.*
But no thought of pain—
no grandeur in pain alone.
For his own grandeur he does not know how to name.

In the Cyrenean cycle Wojtyla writes:

Take a thought if you can—plant its root
in the artisans' hands, in the fingers
of women typing eight hours a day:
black letters hang from reddened eyelids.

Take a thought, make man complete,
or allow him to begin himself anew,
or let him just help You perhaps
and You lead him on.

The idea of the dignity of work is the prevailing theme in the Pope's third encyclical *Laborem Exercens*.

Another notion typical of the Pope's thought is the transforming effect of the spiritual in the life of man. This idea is expressed most clearly in his poems on the Samaritan woman's encounter with Jesus at the well. Thus in his *Song of the Brightness of Water*, he writes:

From this depth—I came only to draw water
in a jug—so long ago, this brightness
still clings to my eyes—the perception I found,
and so much empty space, my own,
reflected in the well.

Yet it is good. I can never take all of you
into me. Stay then as a mirror in the well.
Leaves and flowers remain, and each astonished gaze
brings them down
to my eyes transfixed more by light
than by sorrow.

Pope John Paul II has shown his intense interest in ethical and moral problems and this too is foreshadowed in his poems. Thus he writes in 'The armaments factory worker':

144

Portrait of a Pope

I cannot influence the fate of the globe.
Do I start wars? How can I know
whether I'm for or against?
No, I don't sin.
It worries me not to have influence,
that it is not I who sin.
I only turn screws, weld together
parts of destruction,
never grasping the whole
or the human lot.

I could do otherwise (would parts be left out?)
contributing then to sanctified toil
which no one would blot out in action or belie in speech.
Though what I create is all wrong,
the world's evil is none of my doing.

But is that enough?

During the Second Vatican Council, Bishop Wojtyla wrote a number of explicitly theological poems inspired by the Council and its setting in St Peter's. Typical of this period in his poetry is the poem 'Marble floor':

Our feet meet the earth in this place;
there are so many walls, so many colonnades,
yet we are not lost. If we find
meaning and oneness,
it is the floor that guides us. It joins the spaces
of this great edifice, and joins
the spaces within us,
who walk aware of our weakness and defeat.
Peter, you are the floor, that others
may walk over you (not knowing
where they go). You guide their steps
so that spaces can be one in their eyes,
and from them thought is born.
You want to serve their feet that pass
as rock serves the hooves of sheep.
The rock is a gigantic temple floor,
the cross a pasture.

The final poems to have been published are taken up wholly into the religious sphere. So in *Easter Vigil* (1966) we have 'A conversation with God begins':

145

Portrait of a Pope

The human body in history dies more often and earlier
than the tree.
Man endures beyond the doors of death in catacombs and crypts.
Man who departs endures in those who follow.
Man who follows endures in those departed.
Man endures beyond all coming and going
in himself
and in you.

In this series of poems we find 'Invocation to Man who became the body of history', a poem which foreshadows the Pope's first encyclical, *Redemptor Hominis*:

Oh, Man, in whom our lowest depths meet our heights,
for whom what is within is not a dark burden but the heart.
Man in whom each man can find his deep design,
and the roots of his deeds: the mirror of life and death
staring at the human flux.

THE POPE'S MIND AND TEACHING

The Pope is a theological conservative. In some ways his theological outlook seems to be as narrow as his secular culture is broad. The cast of his mind itself seems to be conservative, and no doubt psychologists would explain this in part by his having had a strict father. A natural conservative leaning in religious matters has been reinforced by the struggle against Communism in Poland. The Polish Church, from which he has sprung, is not so much a reflecting as a confessing Church, clinging understandably to the walls of the Vatican as an ever present help in times of trouble. Rome, from the Polish point of view, is seen not as a threat but as a powerful protector. The Polish Church is also a Church of devotion, with a higher daily mass attendance even than Ireland. In fact, in terms of modern life in the western world, the Polish Church is a magnificent anachronism. The question which has not yet been resolved, is whether the Pope theologically will make the move from Cracow to Rome and appreciate that the responses to Polish Catholic simplicities may not always be appropriate for the complexities of the Universal Church.

Pope John Paul is very much a Pole—he loves his country and is proud of it. With him, in one sense, all roads lead to Warsaw. I recall talking about the English constitution with him and suddenly, with no apparent break in the train of thought, we had passed to the Polish constitution which the Holy Father

pointed out to me was as old as that of England. (I could only recall—though I did not say so—that the Polish constitution had never, because of its individualistic character, worked very well.) This love for his homeland is part of the Pope's make-up. He feels an exile in Rome, however grand and glittering the setting. He misses the mountains and likes to escape from the baroque and the marble as often as he can. No other pope has spent so much time in the summer villa of Castel Gandolfo. He is like a tree rooted in Poland, but with branches spreading out over Europe from the Atlantic to the Urals. His concern for his country is constant and deep. There seems little doubt that were the Russians to invade Poland he would at once return to Poland to protect his people. Poles are outward-looking and their eyes are fixed upon the West while from time to time glancing fearfully over their shoulders to Moscow and the East. Poland explains some of the attitudes which the West, particularly the Catholic intelligentsia, finds puzzling. Catholicism in Poland is clerical hence Pope John Paul's insistence on the importance of ecclesiastical dress. He sees priests and laymen as having distinct roles. Priests should accordingly keep out of politics and laymen out of theology. Again, his conviction that priesthood is exclusively a man's affair springs from his Polish background. One sometimes thinks that the Pope feels that women have no place in the wider male world but should stay with their children in their families, or in their convents.

The abstract nature of the Pope's thought is also a characteristic of Polish intellectual life. His capacity for conceptualization is highly developed and he tends to see things in categories. Thus his approach to married love is both thematic and schematic. He is primarily an ethical philosopher and his rejection of birth control springs from this rigid categorization. In practice, people don't fit into such categories, individuals transcend them. Relationships that do not fit within the parameters of canon law can in fact be loving relationships. Homosexual relationships, for example, can be redeemed by love, as can those between men and women who have irregular unions outside the strict laws of the Church. The Pope seems unwilling to recognize such variations.

One sees the conceptualizing at work again in the Pope's attitude to different countries: France for example is perceived as the eldest daughter of the Church rather than the nation of revolution, equality and the rights of man. The French Catholic tradition after all is balanced by a deep anti-clericalism and in some cases a violent hatred of the Church.

The Pope is conscious of his role of supreme teacher but sometimes in the enunciation of Catholic principles, he seems to ignore the fact that they have to be applied by imperfect men and women. I say 'seems' because as a sensitive and reflecting man he is certainly aware of the problems. Perhaps the key to the contradiction is his consciousness of his office: if the Pope weakens the whole structure of the Church could be shaken. Women in particular seem to be suspicious of his approach to them. The exaltation of Mary hardly compensates for his view that the place of women is in the home. Many find his teaching on birth control harsh and unacceptable.

One can see the particular quality of Pope John Paul's teaching by contrasting his approach with that of his immediate predecessors. John XXIII modified the asperities of moral theology and canon law by his recognition of the uniqueness of each man and woman. Paul VI also exercised a moderating influence through his diffident and almost apologetic approach. He was tortured by the complexities of the problems that faced him. John Paul II is different: he is sure of the truth and validity of traditional Catholic doctrines and their universal applicability. His approach is self-confident and without self-questioning. He preaches his message with panache and enthusiasm, convinced that the world will eventually return to the clarity and simplicity of the Catholic faith. Confidently and joyfully, he is reasserting a Catholic identity.

This approach is seen most clearly in his attitude to priests. He expects much of his priests and appears at times to be rather harsher to them than he is to the laity. His ideal of the Catholic priesthood is summed up in the person and the life of Maximilian Kolbe who was beatified on 17 October 1971. Kolbe was a Franciscan friar who volunteered at Auschwitz in May 1941 to take the place of a married man who had been condemned to starve to death with nine others in a concentration-camp bunker. Father Kolbe was volunteering not only to save the one man, but even more to care pastorally for the other nine. The point was stressed by Cardinal Wojtyla at a press conference after the beatification in Rome. 'It was as a Catholic priest that he accompanied his wretched flock of nine men condemned to death. It was not a question of saving the life of the tenth man—he wanted to help those nine to die. From the moment that the dreadful door clanged shut on the condemned men, he took charge of them, and not just them but others who were dying in cells nearby and whose demented cries caused anyone who approached to shudder. . . . it is a fact that from the moment Father Kolbe came in to their midst, those wretched people felt a protective presence and suddenly their cells in which they awaited the ghastly final dénouement resounded with hymns and prayers.'

Pope John Paul is undoubtedly a compassionate man personally, even if this is not reflected in his official teaching. On one occasion in Cracow he had to rebuke a priest for a fault. He did this comprehensively and even fiercely but having discharged his duty as a bishop, he knelt down and asked the priest to hear his own confession. So by putting himself on the same level as his subject and acknowledging their common status as sinners, he extended a healing hand. What the Pope sees himself as doing in reiterating the traditional principles of Catholic teaching is one of the most difficult things for anyone to do—saying hard things for love. He also wishes to avoid raising false hopes and wants the world to know where he stands. No doubt he recalls that he was elected to consolidate the Church's position after a period of ferment and theological change. The Pope's overriding aim seems to be to preserve the unity and cohesion of the Church, even if that is at the cost of a legitimate pluralism.

Despite these rigidities of principle, Pope John Paul is flexible in dealing with concrete situations. Here, he calls upon his political gifts and is aware of the need to employ checks and balances. Having dealt with the Communist bureaucracy successfully he should not have too much difficulty with that at the Vatican. He also displays a concern for his employees and, as every minister should know, civil servants do in fact respond generously to kindness and consideration. His flexibility was shown in his handling of the synod on the Dutch Church. His presence, even though he remained silent, provided a focus of unity. In the end he did not demand the impossible and the conclusions of the synod were circumscribed by the limits of the practicable. In his dealings with the dissidents Hans Küng and Archbishop Lefebvre he remained firm but always left the door open for future reconciliation and development.

THE PRESENT AND THE FUTURE

The abiding impression Pope John Paul gives is of reality and authenticity. Most of the popes I have known could only have been clerics—they moved in the odour not only of sanctity but of clericalism. What is different about the present pontiff is that one can see him in a variety of roles. He could have been a successful business executive or a leading political figure. It would not be difficult to see him as the father and head of a family. Indeed this was the point made by a middle-aged Polish lady discussing the Pope's attraction for children displayed during his return to Poland, when she remarked: 'This Pope would have been such a good father if he had a wife and family.' The Pope is in a very real sense 'a package deal': it all comes together. A friend, Father Grzybek, sums him up in these words: 'He is a perfect triangle, a man of God, a man of intellect, and a man of great heart.'

Will he grow? Is he a character capable of growth or is his nature cast? Will he have the opportunity to grow? The frailty of his position and his exposure to violence was demonstrated by the sacrilegious attempt on his life last year. Some have seen this as the fulfilment of an alleged prediction by Padre Pio, the Franciscan stigmatist, who is said to have told Father Wojtyla: 'One day you will be pope, but your pontificate will be short and it will end in bloodshed.' (I visited Padre Pio myself in Foggia in southern Italy many years ago. I found him a convincing man and the stigmata were clearly present. The most impressive thing about him was his down-to-earth commonsense approach. At the early morning mass he celebrated in the parish church, one of the pious ladies who surrounded him had gone into a trance when he was distributing Holy Communion. When Padre Pio reached her he gave her a sharp bang on the head with the paten and she immediately came round.)

The answer to the future would appear to lie in the past. Wojtyla has grown with every position he has come to occupy. Starting from the conservative background of the Polish Church, he was able to respond to the Vatican Council, absorbing its spirit and making notable contributions on the subject of the nature of the Church and of religious freedom. He has developed a new concept of the papal role which consists in making himself accessible to people all over the

The Pope preaching at Cologne Cathedral, Germany 1980

world. Yet there are signs that point in in the other direction. He does not appear to respond to what he has found on his travels. Thus he attempted to reassert monogamy in Africa and to enforce his views on contraception in the United States. Questions have been raised about the dynasty to which he truly belongs. Is he in the line of John and Paul or is he in reality Pius XIII? Parallels have been drawn between Pope John Paul's position and that of Pio Nono, the liberal pope who after two years of turmoil and strife abandoned liberalism and followed it by thirty years of reaction.

Will there be scope for the development of Church institutions along collegial lines? There is no doubting the sincerity of the Pope's commitment to the teachings of the Council but his own dominating personality may prevent the development of full collegiality in the Church. He is so extraordinarily forceful that in the presence of such a blazing sun, other prelates have only the light of farthing dips. Furthermore, he has an adamantine will. One example must suffice. He has banned the *sedia gestatoria* (the papal sedan chair) and consigned it to the Vatican lumber room because he cannot bear being carried over the heads of the people with whom he wishes to remain in close contact. The faithful themselves, who under the old dispensation were able to get an unobstructed view of the Holy Father, were not entranced by the new order and a group of them at the beginning of the reign started chanting '*sedia gestatoria*' at him as he walked by. The Pope stopped, turned around to face them, and with swingeing gestures of his right hand declared resolutely: 'No! No! No!' The miscreants subsided.

Will this Pope preside over the reunion of Christendom or will that vision fade as the reign advances? The signs are contradictory but I am not without hope. On the one hand there is the uncompromising reassertion of papal authority together with the upholding of discipline within the Church, both of which have raised Protestant hackles. Not all can share the Pope's deep devotion to Mary. Others are unsympathetic to the strictness of his moral injunctions on such matters as contraception which have passed out of the public Protestant consensus. There is fear for the evangelical principles of tolerance, forgiveness and freedom in the Church of the future.

On the other hand the Pope is undoubtedly committed to the ecumenical movement. Up to 1981 he had made no fewer than eighty-three addresses, long and short, on the subject and he treats it as a matter of urgency. As he declared in Munich on 19 November 1980 at the end of his German visit: 'We do not know how long the way to unity will be. But one thing we know with all the greater certainty; we have to keep on walking this way with courage and perseverance —keep on walking and do not stand still.'

What role will there be for the papacy as such in the enlarged Church of the future? The concept of the papacy formulated by the First Vatican Council is incompatible with ecumenical advance: yet the Second Council enjoins it as a priority duty. The reunion of Christendom, if it is to take place, can do so only around the papacy—no other institution in the Christian world enjoys a comparable history, stature and prestige. But to be acceptable, the doctrine of papal infallibility must be placed in the context of the life of the whole Church—then it could become acceptable to a surprising number.

Rome must stoop to conquer. A papacy seeking to dominate and dictate would repel other Christian Churches and individuals, whereas one willing to listen, to liberate and to serve would draw men and institutions to itself. Which course the papacy follows will be determined above all by the present pope. Perhaps a double role will develop for the papacy: one as head of the Roman Catholic Church as such and a second as a focus of unity for the entire Christian world. These roles might eventually come together but in the beginning they would be distinct although connected.

What of papal influence in the secular world? The Pope sees ecumenism as a part of a wider unity and a contribution towards it. His ultimate concern is with the future of the human race and he fears that a nuclear conflict could break out which would destroy mankind. He prays about this daily and is determined to do everything in his power to avoid a holocaust. It could well be that a reconciling role for the papacy may develop from this commitment and concern.

The Pope may be theologically conservative, but his social thought is firmly on the progressive side. His assertion of human rights against authoritarian Marxism is determined and persistent: it amounts almost to a democratic gospel. At the same time he has a strong distrust of capitalism and dislikes the manifestations of the consumer society. He seems at times to see the materialistic values of the West as constituting as great a threat to man's spirituality as communist autocracy. Perhaps this detachment from ideological commitment will fit him for a mediating role in the future between the forces of capitalism and communism.

The future remains hidden, but it cannot be without hope and promise with such a man as John Paul II playing a major part on the world stage. In the end one comes back to the Pope as a human being. He has the authority not only of his office but of his own integrity and by centering this on the person of Jesus Christ he is the source of immense power and influence. Pope John Paul reasserts the primacy of the spiritual and its ultimate jurisdiction over such objectives as the seeking of security by the amassing of armaments and the pursuit of material wealth. His life and witness calm the fears and anxieties of modern man. As he cried out at his inaugural mass: 'Open wide the doors for Christ. To his saving power open the boundaries of states, economic and political systems, the vast fields of culture, civilization and development. Do not be afraid. Christ knows "what is in man". He alone knows it.'

It is the near-perfect joining and balancing of the human and the religious which gives Pope John Paul his extraordinary appeal. His voice, because it is authentic, penetrates the hearts and minds of both the believer and the unbeliever. By his existence he dignifies both life and man.

Index

Index

Index